PN ST A21

D1718074

ASN.1
The Tutorial and Reference

Abstract Syntax Notation One (ASN.1)
The Tutorial and Reference

Douglas Steedman

TECHNOLOGY APPRAISALS

Technology Appraisals Ltd.

Technology Appraisals is the leading independent company specialising in education and information for users and vendors of computer communications, networking and distributed processing. It provides a wide range of public and private seminars for professional development and training given by international experts, and a range of leading edge publications.

The publications include *OII Spectrum* covering the technologies and markets for open information interchange and document interoperability, and *OSN - Open Systems Networking and Computing* covering computer networking. These monthly information services provide authoritative advice and guidance on key and topical issues and news of market and technical developments. For further information please write or call:

Technology Appraisals Ltd.,
82 Hampton Road, Twickenham, TW2 5QS, United Kingdom.
Tel: +44 81 893 3986, Fax: +44 81 744 1149,
E-mail: techapp@cix.compulink.co.uk

Copyright © Douglas Steedman 1990, 1993

First published in Great Britain 1990
Reprinted with corrections 1993

All rights reserved. No part of this publication may be reproduced, stored in a retrieval system, or transmitted, in any form or by any means, electronic, mechanical, photocopying, recording and/or otherwise, without the prior permission of the publishers.

This book may not be lent, resold, hired out or otherwise disposed of by way of trade in any form of binding or cover other than that in which it was published, without prior consent of the publishers.

BRITISH LIBRARY CATALOGUING-IN-PUBLICATION DATA

Steedman, Douglas
    Abstract Syntax Notation One (ASN.1): The Tutorial and Reference
    1. Computer systems. Programming languages
    I. Title
    005.133

ISBN 1 871802 06 7

Printed and bound in Great Britain

Table of Contents

ASN.1 TUTORIAL   1

ASN.1 REFERENCE   125

Appendices

Preface

ASN.1 has been the internationally standardised way of describing high-level protocol information since 1984, when it was simply known as the X.409 notation. Since then, its specification (and that of its Basic Encoding Rules) has been rewritten, enhancements have been made, and others are planned. It has become a key ingredient of Open Systems Interconnection (OSI). The number of users of the notation, both readers and writers, has increased dramatically, in step with the number of standards and protocols which employ it, and the number of products which implement it.

One thing which hasn't changed so much in that time is the lack of tutorial material available. A few papers have been written, and several general books on OSI feature a section on ASN.1. However, most of these give it a fairly superficial treatment; there are few, if any, comprehensive descriptions.

My aim in writing this book has been to try to fill that gap. The tutorial, which constitutes the main body of the book, covers all of the features of the notation, including the 1988 enhancements and the notorious macro capability, as well as the basic encoding rules. There are also chapters concerned with the fundamental concepts on which ASN.1 is based, its role in OSI, its history and its likely evolution.

The book is intended for anyone who would like to be able to read, write, or speak ASN.1. No specific prior knowledge is demanded of the reader.

It is the job of the standard to specify, as crisply as possible, which sequences of symbols constitute a valid ASN.1 module, and what that module actually denotes. In writing this book, I have set out to complement that specification with explanations and examples, tips and techniques, dos and don'ts, whys and wherefores.

The book also has a number of Appendices which collectively form an ASN.1 reference. The purpose here is not, of course, to compete with the standard, which clearly is definitive, but to present many of the details of ASN.1 in a more reader-friendly way. For example, the Appendices concerned with the syntax of ASN.1 present it in diagrammatic form, each diagram showing some piece of the syntax, with the various pieces presented in alphabetical order for convenient access. Some of the other Appendices gather material in one place which in the standard is widely distributed.

Acknowledgements

While I have participated actively in several OSI standards activities over the past ten years, I think I have felt most gratified by my part in the creation and evolution of ASN.1. True, it has its little quirks and eccentricities, but as a common foundation for all OSI application protocols, it has been and continues to be an important step in the ascent towards the goal of "Open Systems".

Although many people have contributed to ASN.1 over the years, two deserve special mention.

Firstly, there is James E. White, from the U.S.A., former CCITT Special Rapporteur on MHS (Message Handling Systems) and ASN.1, and co-founder of Rapport Communication, Inc.. Jim can legitimately claim to be the creator of ASN.1. In the summer of 1982, he and I independently developed proposals for a general-purpose notation and encoding scheme to be applied to the MHS protocols. We met (for the first time) in Ottawa one weekend, to try to reach a common solution. Fortunately for all concerned, the outcome, which eventually became ASN.1, looked a lot like his proposal, and not so much like mine!

Secondly, there is Professor John Larmouth, of the University of Salford, in the U.K. It was John who was chiefly responsible for bringing CCITT X.409, as it was then, from the field of MHS into the OSI mainstream. He also did the work to separate the notation and encoding, and coined the name "ASN.1". He has continued to be a major technical contributor to the work.

I have greatly enjoyed working with Jim and John and all of the other past and present members of the ASN.1 "team".

I would like to thank Alan Paton of Technology Appraisals for giving me the opportunity to write this book, and David Hitchcock, also of Technology Appraisals, for editorial assistance. I also appreciate the cooperation of my employers, PSC International Limited, and especially the President of PSC, Pat Shea.

I dedicate this my first book to my wife Moira and son Christopher, who have helped in so many ways to make this project possible.

Douglas Steedman
West Linton, Scotland
August, 1990

Notes to the reader

1. Throughout the book, ASN.1 notation is rendered in bold, and in a different typeface from the rest of the text. Thus, for example, the ASN.1 keyword **BOOLEAN** is shown in the way that it is in this sentence. Where an example of ASN.1 taking one or several lines is included in the text, it is enclosed in a box, like this:

```
laguna OCTET STRING ::= 'BEAC'H
```

2. Occasionally, it will be necessary to show a pattern, rather than a specific piece of ASN.1. Such a pattern will include variables rendered in the same typeface as the ASN.1 but not in bold. The actual ASN.1 possibilities can be generated by replacing each variable in the pattern by a valid instance of whatever is suggested by its name. For example, in "**SET OF** Type", the variable "Type" can be replaced by any ASN.1 type.

3. Where examples of encoding are included, hexadecimal notation is normally used, with the digits shown in a further typeface, for example:

$$04 \mid 02 \mid BEAC_{16}$$

The subscripted "16" appears at the end of each line when hexadecimal is used. The box is intended merely to separate visually the different parts of the encoding, and has no further significance.

4. Except in one instance which is clearly noted, the use of ellipsis ("...") within the examples simply indicates that some details which are unnecessary for the understanding of the example have been omitted, and does not form a part of the notation.

5. All terms in the text which have been rendered in **bold** (with the exception of the ASN.1 itself as mentioned above) appear in the glossary of terms.

ASN.1 Tutorial

1 Introduction

This chapter introduces the basic ideas of ASN.1 and the background to its invention.

1.1 What is ASN.1 ?

ASN.1 is the acronym for Abstract Syntax Notation One, a language for describing structured information; typically, information intended to be conveyed across some interface or communication medium. ASN.1 has been standardised internationally. It is widely used in the specification of communication protocols, and in particular, is employed in virtually all of the emerging standards for the application layer of Open Systems Interconnection (OSI).

ASN.1 is reminiscent of a high-level programming language, or at least the data declaration part of such a language. This similarity is not merely a matter of appearance: ASN.1 brings to the field of protocol specification many of the benefits that high-level languages brought to the world of programming. Prior to ASN.1, information to be conveyed in communication protocols was typically specified by ascribing meanings to particular bits and bytes in protocol messages, much as programmers, before the advent of high level languages, had to deal with the bits and bytes of storage layout.

With ASN.1, the protocol designer can view and describe the relevant information and its structure at a high level and need not be unduly concerned with how it is represented while in transit. Indeed, it may well be that under different circumstances, the information is in fact represented in different ways (this possibility is manifested in OSI by the existence of the Presentation Layer).

ASN.1 comes into its own when the information being described is complex. This is because the language allows arbitrarily complex structures to be built up in a uniform way from simpler components, and ultimately from a few simple information types.

Given any ASN.1 description of a message, a representation can be derived mechanically by applying a set of encoding rules. While many such sets could be imagined, a single set, the Basic Encoding Rules (BER), has been standardised, as a companion standard to ASN.1 itself.

1.2 ASN.1 history

ASN.1 was first standardised in 1984 by the International Telegraph and Telephone Consultative Committee (CCITT) in its Recommendation X.409, and was at first referred to simply as "the X.409 notation". The term "Abstract Syntax Notation One" was coined later, on its adoption by the International Organisation for Standardisation (ISO). While the notation had no direct predecessors in the standards world, it drew some inspiration from the "Courier" notation, invented by Xerox Corporation, and used in specifying its XNS suite of protocols.

The need for a standard specification language for protocol information was first observed during CCITT's trail-blazing electronic mail standardisation activity of 1980-1984, known as Message Handling Systems (MHS). This activity led to the X.400-series of Recommendations, and X.409, created in support of MHS, was nominally a part of this series.[1] In practice, X.409 was completely independent of the MHS application it was born to serve.

Many of the information objects inherent in MHS are structurally very complex. For example, an electronic mail message as submitted to the MHS is composed of an "envelope" and a "contents" (by analogy with the postal service). An envelope, in turn, includes descriptions of the intended recipients of the message, together with any actions the MHS is requested to take, or has taken, on the message. Some of the requests are associated with individual recipients, others common to them all. A recipient is described by, *inter alia*, an "O/R Name", which is itself a structured information item, names being made up of "attributes".

Faced with this complexity, the MHS group defined a notation for specifying complex information structures: the X.409 notation. Also specified in X.409, and at that time considered to be closely associated with it, were what later became known as the BER, but which at the time were simply known as "X.409 encoding".

Shortly after X.409 was defined, various other groups standardising OSI applications found that it was suitable for their needs also (to no surprise of the MHS group). ISO, however, which housed several of these activities, was unhappy with the coupling of the notation and encoding aspects, and split X.409 into two separate documents along these lines.

---

[1]   Recommendation X.409, "Message handling systems: presentation transfer syntax and notation", CCITT Red Book, Fascicle VIII.7, International Telecommunications Union, October 1984, pp 62-93

The first aspect, the notation, was named "Abstract Syntax Notation One" or simply "ASN.1".[2] The term "abstract syntax" is that employed in OSI to denote application layer information considered divorced from its representation. The "One" was added by ISO to leave open the future possibility of a better language for expressing abstract syntaxes. None has been found, however, and indeed no strong requirement to search for one has been encountered. An "ASN.2", should it ever be considered necessary, will have to provide significantly more powerful capability than ASN.1 to be worth inventing.

The second aspect was termed the "Basic Encoding Rules". Again, the name results from ISO keeping an eye to the future, when other sets of encoding rules may be standardised. Such additional standardised encoding rules will not be different from BER for difference's sake, but will be based upon meeting some significantly different need, for example, optimising compactness of representation. (Of course there is nothing to prevent private organisations defining their own non-standard encoding rules for any reasons whatever).

CCITT agreed back in 1985 to work collaboratively with ISO on this subject, and to adopt, as the basis for this work, the two ISO documents, as well as the names ASN.1 and BER.

ISO finally published the two documents as ISO 8824 and ISO 8825 in 1987.[3,4] Technically they were very close to X.409. (The main difference was the addition of three new types of character string and two "useful" types).

In the meantime, a number of further extensions to the capabilities of X.409 were being developed and agreed collaboratively between ISO and CCITT.

CCITT was first to publish the outcome of this work, as its Recommendations X.208 and X.209.[5,6] At the time of writing, the

---

2   The dot (".") in "ASN.1" was introduced at the request of the U.S.A. to prevent the acronym being mistaken for that of the American National Standards Institute (ANSI), although it was never clear in what context they could be confused!

3   ISO 8824:1987, "Information Processing Systems - Open Systems Interconnection - Specification of Abstract Syntax Notation (ASN.1)", International Organization for Standardization, 1987

4   ISO 8825:1987, "Information Processing Systems - Open Systems Interconnection - Specification of Basic Encoding Rules for Abstract Syntax Notation (ASN.1)", International Organization for Standardization, 1987

5   Recommendation X.208, "Open systems interconnection: specification of Abstract Syntax Notation (ASN.1)", CCITT Blue Book, Fascicle VIII.4, International Telecommunications Union, Geneva 1989, pp 57-130

corresponding revised versions of ISO 8824 and ISO 8825 are still in the publication process.

In 1988, ISO merged its information technology standards activity with that of another standards organisation, the International Electrotechnical Commission (IEC), forming a joint technical committee called ISO/IEC JTC1. All OSI activities, including ASN.1 are now handled by JTC1, rather than ISO.

The collaboration on ASN.1 between CCITT and (now) JTC1 is continuing, and further enhancements are likely. Chapter 9 describes a number of the possibilities under consideration.

---

6   Recommendation X.209, "Open systems interconnection: specification of Basic Encoding Rules for Abstract Syntax Notation (ASN.1)", *ib. id.,* pp 131-151

2 Abstract and Transfer Syntax

This chapter introduces the notions of abstract and transfer syntax.

2.1 Information and data

It has frequently been observed that the difference between information and data is that the former is what results when the latter have been interpreted in some context. The word "information" has a connotation of meaningfulness whereas "data" does not. Thus it has been said that a collection of temperature and pressure readings from various locations constitutes (raw) data, whereas a weather forecast extracted from those readings constitutes information. This view certainly holds as far as human beings are concerned. On the other hand, the readings themselves are considered as information by the forecasting software.

It all depends on viewpoint, and the concepts of information and data are therefore relative.

Nonetheless, in the protocol context, we are concerned with the notion of **data** as the uninterpreted bits or octets conveyed between systems by some transfer mechanism. The purpose of sending this data is to convey meanings between the systems: these meanings constitute the **information** being conveyed.

In OSI one important data transfer mechanism involved is the session service; its service primitives provide for the conveyance of user data (this is also true of all lower layers). At the Presentation Layer, however, there is a transition, reflecting the role of that layer. Its services (and those of higher level services) provide for the conveyance of user *information*.

This transition is supported by the concepts of abstract and transfer syntax.

2.2 Abstract and transfer syntax

To illustrate the concepts of abstract and transfer syntax, consider an unmanned meteorological station, which, either on request or periodically, reports on the prevailing atmospheric conditions to a

7

monitoring centre. At the monitoring centre, the information is input to a weather forecasting program.[7]

We assume that some communication path is in place which allows the station to send data to the central computer, and will not concern ourselves further with how these data are actually conveyed. This is a problem for lower level protocols (in OSI, layers 1 to 4) and may involve communications media such as data networks, radio nets, satellites, telephone lines, telex, and functions such as multiplexing, error detection, retransmission, segmentation, and so on.

We are concerned solely with the information conveyed between the application programs running in the computers at the weather station and the monitoring centre.

For different reasons, both programs need to 'know' what information is included in a report. The application in the weather station needs to know in order that it can synthesise the report from the appropriate sensor readings. The application in the centre needs to know because it must be able to analyse reports, for example so as to be able to revise its forecasts if the atmospheric pressure changes.

This knowledge, which is essential for the programs to be written, is that of the **abstract syntax**; the set of all possible (distinct) reports. The designer of the abstract syntax also defines the meaning of each possible report, and this allows the developers of the programs at each end to implement the appropriate actions.

It would be very unusual for a designer to define the abstract syntax of a message type by explicitly listing all possible messages. This is because any realistic message type will allow a very large number of distinct possibilities. Instead, the abstract syntax will generally be structured. The set of possible messages and their meanings can then be inferred from knowledge of the possibilities for each of the components of the structure.

This is true of the example at hand. As an informal description of the abstract syntax, let us say that each report contains the following information:

-    station number (1-99999);
-    time and date of report (YYMMDDHHMMSS);
-    barometric pressure (millibars);
-    temperature (degrees Celsius);
-    relative humidity (%);
-    average wind velocity (kmh-1);
-    average wind direction (units of 7.5° from true north).

---

[7]   The author has no specialised knowledge of this application, so it is highly unlikely that this example has any resemblance to the way that this problem is dealt with in reality.

It can be seen that the number of possible distinct reports is enormous (of the order of 10^{25}). However, this situation is manageable because each report is structured into a modest number of components, each of which is itself manageable.

While shared knowledge of the abstract syntax is necessary for the meaningful exchange of information between application programs, it is not in itself sufficient. It is also necessary for agreement on the **transfer syntax**: the way that each of the possible messages is represented as a string of octets. (Or bits or characters or whatever unit of transfer the underlying communication service provides). Corresponding to any abstract syntax there are an arbitrary number of possible transfer syntaxes.

As one possibility for the abstract syntax described above, we could have a fixed format message, something like:

Octets	Represent	
1-3	station number	(5 BCD digits; last semi-octet unused)
4	year	(2 BCD digits)
5	month	(2 BCD digits)
6	day	(2 BCD digits)
7	hour	(2 BCD digits)
8	minute	(2 BCD digits)
9	second	(2 BCD digits)
10-11	pressure	(4 BCD digits)
12	temperature (sign)	(all 0s for +; all 1s for -)
13	temperature (magnitude)	(2 BCD digits)
14-15	humidity	(3 BCD digits; last semi-octet unused)
16-17	average wind velocity	(3 BCD digits; last semi-octet unused)
18	average wind direction	(2 BCD digits)

BCD here stands for binary coded decimal, a two-level scheme in which a number is represented as a whole in decimal but each decimal digit is represented in binary. Since 4 bits (well actually a little over 3 bits) are needed to represent a decimal digit, an octet can hold two of them. In each semi-octet, the digits are represented in their obvious way, so that the digit 0 is represented by 0000, the digit 1 by 0001, and so on. The values 1010, 1011, 1100, 1101, 1110, and 1111 are unused.

The following shows, in hexadecimal form, a weather report encoded using this transfer syntax:

7329009001021257031056FF0302600015000$_{16}$

An alternative possibility would be to use a character-based encoding. This would be particularly appropriate where the underlying communications medium is itself character-based, as with Telex, for example. Here, all information is first represented as a character string, then the individual characters are themselves represented by suitable codes, such as those of ASCII.

With a character-based encoding for some abstract syntax such as that in the example above, it is normal for only certain character strings to represent valid messsages. Thus, the character string:

"treon ther were, ful of frut, wel thikke on everich bough"

is unlikely to correspond to a valid weather report. The character strings which are valid messages can be described by a grammar, using a notation such as Backus-Naur Form (BNF). BNF has been widely used to define the syntax of programming languages since it was used to define Algol 60. It is also used to define ASN.1.

For example, the following grammar describes a valid character-based transfer syntax for the weather report example:

Report	=	{ StationNumber ; DateAndTime ; Pressure ; Temperature ; Humidity ; WindVelocity ; WindDirection }
StationNumber	=	PositiveNumber
DateAndTime	=	Year Month Day Hour Minute Second
Pressure	=	PositiveNumber
Temperature	=	Number
Humidity	=	PositiveNumber
WindVelocity	=	PositiveNumber
WindDirection	=	PositiveNumber
Year	=	TwoDigits
Month	=	TwoDigits
Day	=	TwoDigits
Hour	=	TwoDigits
Minute	=	TwoDigits
Second	=	TwoDigits
TwoDigits	=	Digit Digit
PositiveNumber	=	NonZeroDigit DigitSequence | Digit
DigitSequence	=	Digit DigitSequence | Digit
Number	=	PositiveNumber | - PositiveNumber
Digit	=	**0** | NonZeroDigit
NonZeroDigit	=	**1** |**2** |**3** |**4** |**5** |**6** |**7** |**8** |**9**

In the variant of BNF used here, **bold** is used to render symbols that actually appear in the allowed strings, as opposed to those used in defining the grammar.

In this example, the various numbers representing the fields have been allowed to be of variable length, with a separator (";") showing where one number ends and another begins. We could equally have opted for fixed-length fields (as in the previous example) in which case no separator would be needed. Similarly we have chosen to convey the fields in a fixed order, whereas we could have allowed variable order, in which case we would have had to arrange for the fields to be self-identifying.

Anyway, given this grammar, the example report shown above is represented by the following character string:

{73290;900102125703;1056;-3;26;15;0}

which in hexadecimal, where the characters are ASCII-coded with null parity, is:

$7B37333239303B39303031303231323535373 0_{16}$
$333B313035363B2D333B32363B31353B307D_{16}$

It turns out that the latter transfer syntax takes precisely twice as many (36 rather than 18) octets to represent the example. The dominant factor at work here is the use of an entire octet rather than a semi-octet to represent a decimal digit. The primary advantage of the latter is that the report can be directly displayed on a suitable terminal without any need for translation.

In both of these encoding approaches, the formulation of the transfer syntax is a creative act, with decisions needed on issues such as the representation of numbers, the separation of fields, and so on. These decisions are not *in essence* specific to the weather report example. It would seem preferrable that such decisions be taken once (or possibly a very few times) in a general-purpose way. A set of **encoding rules** is a consistent and complete set of such decisions, allowing the systematic derivation of a transfer syntax from an abstract syntax.

The encoding rules approach to transfer syntax definition results in considerable saving of effort for application protocol designers. This is particularly pronounced where the messages involved are complex. Perhaps even more important then the savings to the designers are the potential savings to implementors through the ability to develop general-purpose run-time support. Thus, for example, encoding and decoding subroutines can be developed once and then used in a wide range of applications.

A set of encoding rules can only be developed in the context of an agreed set of concepts available to the designers of abstract syntaxes. For example, the concepts required in designing the weather report abstract syntax included the ability to create a message from a sequence of fields, and the concepts of integer and whole number (restricted to certain ranges).

Such a set of concepts have been agreed internationally, and are available to the designer in the form of a language for abstract syntax specification. This language is of course ASN.1, the subject of this book.

Using ASN.1, the example abstract syntax can be expressed thus:

```
WeatherReport ::= SEQUENCE
{
    stationNumber     INTEGER (1..99999),
    timeOfReport      UTCTime,
    pressure          INTEGER (850..1100),
    temperature       INTEGER (-100..60),
    humidity          INTEGER (0..100),
    windVelocity      INTEGER (0..500),
    windDirection     INTEGER (0..48)
}
```

ASN.1 also allows particular values to be specified; this capability is used mostly for writing down examples. The particular report which was used to illustrate the transfer syntaxes above is:

```
{
    stationNumber     73290,
    timeOfReport      "900102125703Z",
    pressure          1056,
    temperature       -3,
    humidity          26,
    windVelocity      15,
    windDirection     0
}
```

Also internationally agreed and available for use are the Basic Encoding Rules (BER) which allow the automatic derivation of a transfer syntax for every abstract syntax defined using ASN.1. Transfer syntaxes produced by application of the BER can be used over any communications medium which allows the transfer of strings of octets, such as the OSI session service.

One possible BER encoding of the example weather report (there are options, so a number of encodings are possible) is as follows:

$30240203011E4A170D3930303130323132353737_{16}$
$3033590202042000201FD02011A02010F02010016_{16}$

(I will explain in Chapter 6 how that can be derived). The total length here is 38 octets, roughly the same as with the character-based transfer syntax. However, the BER encoding carries information in a form that is more convenient and efficient for machine processing. Also, as will be shown later, the BER encoding rules are much more flexible, and scale up easily to complex examples.

3 Basics of ASN.1

This chapter describes the basic concepts and syntactic constructs of ASN.1, including types, values, subtypes and modules. It also describes the naming of various objects of ASN.1 and the referencing of definitions from other modules and from text.

3.1 Types and values

ASN.1 is a language for specifying abstract syntax. Loosely speaking, this means that it is used to describe the structure and information content of messages, such as those which might be exchanged between application processes.

In this regard, the fundamental concepts of ASN.1 are the inter-related notions of **type** and **value**. A type is a (non-empty) set of values, and represents a potential for conveying information. Only values are actually conveyed, but their type governs the domain of possibilities. It is by selecting one particular value of the type, rather than the others, that the sender of a message conveys information. The type may have only a few values, and therefore be capable of conveying only a few distinctions. An example of such a type is Boolean, which has only the two values true and false, with nothing in between. On the other hand, some types, such as Integer and Real, have a (countably) infinite number of values and can thus express arbitrarily fine distinctions.

A type is a **subtype** of another, its **parent (type)**, if its values are a subset of those of the parent. Thus, for example, a type "whole number", whose values are the non-negative integers, could be defined as a subtype of Integer. (ASN.1 does not provide such a type, but one could be defined by the user if needed).

A type may be simple or structured. The **simple types** are the basic building blocks of ASN.1, and include types like Boolean and integer. A simple type will generally be used to describe a single aspect of something. A **structured type**, on the other hand, is defined in terms of other types - its components - and its values are made up of values of the component types. Each of these components may itself be simple or structured, and this nesting can proceed to an arbitrary depth, to suit the needs of the application. All structured types are ultimately defined in terms of simple types.

An abstract syntax can be defined as a type, normally a structured type. Its values are precisely the set of valid messages under that abstract syntax. Should the messages be structured, as they commonly are, into fields, then the various fields themselves are defined as types. The values of such a type, in turn, are the set of permitted contents of that field.

ASN.1 makes available to the abstract syntax designer a number of simple types, as well as techniques for defining structured types and subtypes. The designer employs these types by using the **type notation** which ASN.1 provides for each such type. ASN.1 also provides **value notation** which allows arbitrary values of these types to be written down.

Any type (or indeed value) which can be written down can be given a name by which it can be referenced. This allows users to define and name types and values that are useful within some enterprise or sphere of interest. These **defined types** (or **defined values**) can then be made available for use by others. The defined types within some enterprise can be seen as supplementing the **built-in types** - those provided directly by ASN.1. ASN.1 also provides a small number of **useful types**, types which have been defined in terms of the built-in types but which are potentially of use across a wide range of enterprises.

A type is defined by means of a type assignment, and a value is defined by a value assignment.

A **type assignment** has three syntactic components: the type reference (the name being allocated to the new type); the symbol "::=", which can be read as "is defined as"; and the appropriate type notation. For example:

```
WeatherReport ::= SEQUENCE
{
      stationNumber      INTEGER (1..99999),
      timeOfReport       UTCTime,
      pressure           INTEGER (850..1100),
      temperature        INTEGER (-100..60),
      humidity           INTEGER (0..100),
      windVelocity       INTEGER (0..500),
      windDirection      INTEGER (0..48)
}
```

defines a type called **WeatherReport**. Everything following the "::=" constitutes valid type notation (for a structured type which comprises a sequence of simple types).

A **value assignment** is similar, but has an additional syntactic component: the type to which the value belongs. This appears between the value reference (the name being allocated to the value), and the "::=". For example:

```
sampleReport WeatherReport ::=
{
        stationNumber      73290,
        timeOfReport       "900102125703Z",
        pressure           1056,
        temperature        -3,
        humidity           26,
        windVelocity       15,
        windDirection      0
}
```

defines a value of type **WeatherReport** called **sampleReport**. The characters after the "::=" constitute valid notation for a value of **WeatherReport**.

The definition of types and values is almost the only thing that ASN.1 users do. Of these two, the definition of types predominates. This is because an abstract syntax itself is a type, as are its components, and *their* components, and so on. In a specification, it is the types, the sets of possible values, which are most significant. Individual values only appear as examples and defaults. Consider how much more useful in a specification is the type **INTEGER** than the particular value **314** (or any other integer value for that matter). Conversely, in instances of communication it is values which are significant.

3.2   Subtypes

Frequently the designer intends only some subset of the values of an ASN.1 type to be valid in some situation. For instance, in conveying a measure of humidity as a percentage, only numbers in the range 0 to 100 are valid, or when conveying a postal code only strings with certain characters and whose length falls within a certain range are to be permitted. Perhaps when some protocol message is used in a certain context, the optional checksum field is to be absent.

These are all examples of constraints which can be expressed by defining a subtype of a suitable parent type. This is done by appending to the notation for the parent a suitable **subtype specification**. The result is itself a type and can be used anywhere a type is allowed. (Thus a subtype specification can also be applied to a subtype, in which case it may serve to further reduce the set of values).

A subtype specification consists of one or more **subtype value
sets**, separated by "|" (pronounced "or"). The whole list is in round
brackets (()).

For example in:

```
Weekend ::= DaysOfTheWeek (saturday | sunday)
```

the type **Weekend** is defined by appending a subtype specification to
a parent type **DaysOfTheWeek**. The subtype specification (the
expression in round brackets) defines which of the values of
DaysOfTheWeek are also to be values of **Weekend**.

Each value set defines some subset of the values of the parent
type. The resulting subtype has the values in the union of these
subsets, which must be non-empty.

There are six different value set notations. Two of these are
applicable to all parent types, others to only certain parent types.
Appendix E shows the dependency.

The value set notations that are applicable to all parent types are
single value and **contained subtype**. The former notation is
simply some value of the parent type, the resulting value set
consisting of that value alone. Examples of this are "**saturday**" and
"**sunday**" above, each of which is a single value of **DaysOfTheWeek**.
The contained subtype notation comprises the keyword **INCLUDES**,
followed by some other subtype of the same parent type, and denotes
the value set consisting of all of the values in that subtype.

For example, given:

```
LongWeekend ::= DaysOfTheWeek
            (INCLUDES Weekend | monday)
```

the type **LongWeekend** includes the three values **saturday**, **sunday**,
and **monday**, the union of the value sets used in its definition.

As mentioned above, the remaining value set notations are specific
to certain parent types, so I will just overview them here and describe
them in detail in Chapter 4 along with the first type for which they
apply.

The **value range** notation can be used to subtype any type
whose values are ordered (for example, the integer type). It involves
specifying the lower and upper bounds of the range.

A **size range** can be included for any type whose values have a
defined size (for example, the bit string type).[8] Here the value set
includes all of the values whose size, measured in the appropriate
units, is within the designated range.

An **alphabet limitation** can be applied only to character string
types and allows only the values formed from some subset of the
characters.

---

[8]   The size is in terms of the abstract value, not the encoded value.

Finally, **inner subtyping** can be employed to define value sets of structured types (for example, set and set-of types). Here the value set includes all those values whose component values meet certain constraints.

3.3 Names

Several categories of object in ASN.1 have names by which they can be referenced. Defined types and values are among them, and their names are called **references**. The components of various types can also be given names. These names are **identifiers**. We have actually met examples of each of these kinds of name above, as follows:

type reference:	**WeatherReport**
value reference:	**sampleReport**
identifier:	**humidity**

It is very important that names are chosen, as in these examples, to have significance to the human reader. Indeed, if names are chosen correctly (and appropriate layout conventions followed), then the essence of some piece of ASN.1 can often be grasped, even by someone unskilled in the language.

All names in ASN.1 are character strings drawn from the same set of characters, namely:

upper-case letters:	**ABCDEFGHIJKLMNOPQRSTUVWXYZ**
lower-case letters:	**abcdefghijklmnopqrstuvwxyz**
decimal digits:	**0123456789**
hyphen:	**-**

The first character in a name must be a letter. A hyphen cannot be the last character in a name, and cannot be immediately followed by another hyphen. The case of the letters in a name is significant, so that "**borders**" and "**Borders**" are different names. In fact the case of the initial letter is of special significance, as type references (and also module references, see below) must start with an upper-case letter, while value references and identifiers must start with a lower-case letter. It is not a good idea, however, to use two or more names which differ only by the case of some of their letters.

The names chosen by users must be chosen so as to avoid clashing with the reserved words of ASN.1 (which include most of the keywords of the language). Since the keywords are generally in upper-case, the use of lower-case letters in names makes it easy to adhere to this, and also generally makes the names more readable. There is no upper limit on the length of names, and this allows the use of an appropriate phrase as the name of an object. Of course, excessively long names actually work against readability.

Examples of legal (and probably appropriate) names are:

UnformattedPostalAddress
Access-control-list
ACL
Temperature
MverifyPDU
recordLow
lb-g3facsimile-non-basic-parameters

The first few of these examples are valid for use as type references, the others as identifiers or value references.

Notice that two different conventions are used in these examples for forming multi-word names, since spaces are not valid in names and thus can not be used to separate the individual words. One approach is to capitalise the first letter (only) of each word (except possibly the first). The other is to use hyphens as separators. Both conventions are in wide use and are equally valid. Normally a particular designer will have a preference, and will use that convention consistently. The preference of this author is for the first of these, and henceforth that will be used in the examples.

Examples of legal (but probably inappropriate) names are:

XYZ
X147-119-2A
Fubar
TheGroundTemperatureExpressedInDegreesCelsius
ACCESSCONTROLLIST
sampleweatherreport
mumble

Character sequences which cannot be used as names (despite being composed of valid characters) include:

1560
3M
access--control--list
T-
relative humidity
OBJECT

(The final example is a reserved word).

3.4 Modules

Any designer can freely define (and name) types and values, and will often allocate references which other designers have also allocated (for their own purposes). How, therefore, can one ensure that when a name is used the intended definition is referred to? Within what scope does a designer have to ensure uniqueness of references? The answer is that a type or value definition does not stand alone but is instead part of a **module**. The module is the basis for organising definitions in ASN.1.

A module is a named collection of definitions of types and values (and macros). A module normally groups together a set of related definitions, such as all those used in defining some abstract syntax. However, the basis for grouping definitions into modules is entirely in the hands of the designer, who could put all definitions into one module, or organise them into several modules, according to taste.

Within a module, definitions can appear in any order, with none of the restrictions sometimes found in programming languages, such as "define before use". It is up to the designer to organise the definitions to make the result most understandable to the reader.

All types and values defined in a single module must be allocated distinct references, and within the module such a reference unambiguously identifies the applicable type or value.

A module consists of, in order: the module identifier; the keyword **DEFINITIONS**; optionally, the tag style default; the symbol "::="; the module body. The module body consists of the exports and imports statements, if any, followed by the type and value assignments, all enclosed between **BEGIN** and **END**.

We will return later to the tag style default (in 4.2.6) and the exports and imports statements (3.4), each of which in any case is optional. An example of a module, in which all of these components are omitted, is as follows:

```
WeatherReporting {2 6 6 247 1} DEFINITIONS ::=
BEGIN
     WeatherReport ::= SEQUENCE { ... }
     sampleReport WeatherReport ::= { ... }
END
```

The module identifier (which precedes the keyword **DEFINITIONS**) constitutes the complete and unambiguous identification of the module. It consists of two components, the first a module reference and the second an object identifier value; in the example they are **WeatherReporting** and **{2 6 6 247 1}** respectively.

A module reference is the same (syntactically) as a type reference, made up of the usual name-forming characters of ASN.1, the first of which must be an upper-case letter. The module reference should be chosen so as to be suggestive of the contents of the module in some way, and, if possible, unambiguous.

The other component, the object identifier value, is a globally unique identification for the module, made up of a sequence of non-negative numbers. We will get round to the subject of object identifiers in a later chapter. While the object identifier value is optional, this is largely for backwards compatibility reasons, because it was not present in the first version of ASN.1. In practice it is not a good idea to omit it.

3.4 Exports and imports

While some modules may be complete and self-contained, it is more normal for modules to need to refer to types and/or values which are defined in others. For example, one module may be a library of general-purpose definitions which are to be used in various abstract syntaxes. This inter-module referencing is accomplished through the ASN.1 import and export capabilities, and, in exceptional cases, through external references.

The author of a module indicates that a definition is available for use elsewhere by **export**ing its reference. If a definition is not exported, then it cannot legally be used anywhere except in that module.

An explicit exports statement can be included in the module, listing the references of any definitions which are to be available for use elsewhere. If no such statement is included, the exports list is considered to contain all of the references defined in the module; that is, the default is to export everything.

An exports statement consists of the keyword **EXPORTS** followed by any references (type, value, or macro) to be exported. The references are separated by commas, and the whole statement is terminated by a semi-colon.

For the example module above to export **WeatherReport** and **sampleReport**, the following exports list could be included, after the **BEGIN**:

```
EXPORTS WeatherReport, sampleReport;
```

In this instance the same effect could be achieved by including no exports statement. This may be useful for a module forming a library of definitions, as it avoids the error-prone task of having to create a long exports list including all of the type references in the module.

If no definitions are to be exported, this is indicated by means of:

```
EXPORTS ;
```

The author of a module which is to make use of an exported definition **import**s it, by including the appropriate reference, together with the module identifier (of the exporting module), in the module's imports statement. The reference can then be used within the (importing) module, and refers to the exported definition.

An imports statement consists of the keyword **IMPORTS**, followed by a list of references for each exporting module from which a definition is to be imported. Each such list is followed by the keyword **FROM** and the module identifier of the exporting module.

For example, a module which needed to make use of **WeatherReport** and **sampleReport** might include the following imports statement:

```
IMPORTS    ...
               WeatherReport, sampleReport
                       FROM WeatherReporting {2 6 6 247 1}
           ...;
```

The ellipses show where lists of references from other modules could be included, if necessary.

The whole imports statement is, like the exports statement, terminated by a semi-colon.[9] Where there is an imports statement, it appears after the exports statement, if any, and before the rest of the module body.

The module identifier following the keyword **FROM** is that which appeared at the head of the exporting module. The reason for the inclusion of the object identifier, as a globally unambiguous identifier, can now be seen. In its absence there is no assurance that an imports statement properly identifies the exporting module, because the module reference is just a text string which could easily have been independently chosen by several module authors.

Once a reference has been included in the imports statement, it can then be used freely within the module. However, occasionally, a situation arises where an explicit **external reference** is needed. Such a reference is formed by prefixing the type or value reference with the module reference of the exporting module, and separating them by a period (".").

For example, were an external reference needed for **sampleReport**, it would be:

```
WeatherReporting.sampleReport
```

In the first version of ASN.1, which did not provide for export or import lists, this was the only way to cross-reference among modules. While ASN.1 still allows such external references, it is recommended that they only be used when two or more definitions with the same reference have been imported (from different exporting modules, of course).

---

9   Consideration is presently being given to changing the definition of ASN.1 so that all statements, including type and value assignments, are terminated with a semi-colon. This is discussed further in 9.1.

3.5   Layout of ASN.1 modules

ASN.1 imposes virtually no constraints over the layout of an ASN.1 module. In particular, any two syntactic items may be separated by an arbitrary amount of white-space (spaces, tabs, and newlines), and comments. Individual syntactic items, however, like names, keywords, and symbols such as "::=" must not be interrupted by white-space or comments.

A comment is a syntactic device for including text of any kind within an ASN.1 module.

The start of a comment is indicated by a pair of hyphens, and its end by a matching pair of hyphens, or by the end of a line, whichever comes first. (This is the single place in ASN.1 where an end of line is significant and considered different from the other forms of white-space). In printed specifications, it is common for the contents of a comment to be displayed in a smaller typeface than the ASN.1, and italicised. Such typographical conventions have no impact, however, on the interpretation of the notation.

In fact, typography is not significant anywhere in ASN.1. Nonetheless, it can be important from the viewpoint of readability. It is particular helpful if ASN.1 is rendered differently from any surrounding text.

The use of white-space can also be a considerable aid to readability. Take the definition of **WeatherReport** from above, reproduced here:

```
WeatherReport ::= SEQUENCE
{
        stationNumber     INTEGER (1..99999),
        timeOfReport      UTCTime,
        pressure          INTEGER (850..1100),
        temperature       INTEGER (-100..60),
        humidity          INTEGER (0..100),
        windVelocity      INTEGER (0..500),
        windDirection     INTEGER (0..48)
}
```

this employs a number of layout conventions, including the lining up of matching brackets, and the components of the structure. The exact details are a matter of taste. The following, however, defines the same type, and should, of course, be avoided:

```
WeatherReport ::= SEQUENCE{stationNumber INTEGER
(1..99999),timeOfReport UTCTime,pressure INTEGER
(850..1100),temperature INTEGER (-100..60),humidity
INTEGER (0..100),windVelocity INTEGER
(0..500),windDirection INTEGER (0..48)}
```

3.6 ASN.1 in specifications

ASN.1 allows the designer to specify some, but not all, aspects of a distributed application. For example, there is no way to express the *meaning* of particular data types and values, except by the choice of "meaningful" names, which is clearly inadequate in general. Behavioural aspects are also not covered. Such things will therefore have to be expressed in some other way, such as by natural language, formal description techniques, state diagrams, flow charts, or some combination of these. For the specification to be complete, it will be necessary for this to be linked in in some way with the ASN.1.

Presently, in OSI standards, the linkage is through the association of natural language text with the ASN.1.[10]

The most restricted way is through the embedding of text within ASN.1, by means of the comment facility.

The comment facility is appropriate for attaching short text qualifiers to particular definitions. In fact, the ASN.1 specification itself mandates the use of comments in a few particular places where the notation itself does not allow something to be expressed. (The number of places where this is necessary has diminished, and hopfefully will drop to zero as ASN.1 is enhanced). However, the use of comments is not adequate for any more substantial specification.

The problem then is one of being able to refer to the ASN.1 definitions from the text. Generally, this can be done by use, within the text, of the reference names and identifiers in the ASN.1. The fact that such words are actually pointers into the ASN.1 is often emphasised by the consistent use of a different typeface for the ASN.1 names (as is done in this book).

In fact, for expository purposes, it is often helpful for entire definitions, not just names, to appear embedded in text. For example it may be helpful in a protocol specification to show a type assignment at the point in the text which describes the meaning of that type.

---

[10] Work is getting under way in the standards groups to define linkages between ASN.1 and some formal description techniques (FDTs), notably ACT ONE, an algebraic specification language which is part of the standard FDT, LOTOS.

The following example is drawn from the OSI directory specification:

> ... unless the **returnCrossRefs** component of the corresponding request had the value **TRUE**. This component consists of a sequence of **CrossReference** items, each of which contains a **contextPrefix** and an **accessPoint** descriptor (see 12.8).
>
> ```
> CrossReference ::= SET
> {
>         contextPrefix          [0]          DistinguishedName,
>         accessPoint            [1]          AccessPoint
> }
> ```
>
> A **CrossReference** may be added by a DSA when it matches part of the **targetObject** argument ...

However, an assignment on its own, such as that of **CrossReference**, is not really a valid unit of ASN.1 to find in a specification, the valid unit being the module. Such an assignment must therefore considered merely to be an extract from the definitive module, which must appear, complete and intact, somewhere in the specification. This is the case with the OSI Directory example, in which the complete module can be found in an annex. It is there alone that the module header appears, including the imports and exports.

Instead of an annex or appendix, some other standards hold their complete module in a figure possibly spread over several pages. The FTAM protocol standard uses a series of figures, one on each of 12 consecutive pages. In addition, every line in the module has a line number (1-714) and this provides the basis for a complete cross-reference of all of the definitions, which is done in an informative annex.

Another approach to embedding definitions at appropriate places in text has been used in some standards, and may occasionally be encountered. It involves splitting the module up into many fragments, each syntactically valid as a module, but all bearing the same module reference. Each such fragment typically contains a single definition, and it is these fragments that are actually embedded in the text. Although this approach is presently allowed, it should be avoided, since the complete module never appears together. This usage will probably be made invalid by a future revision of ASN.1.

4 ASN.1 Types

This chapter introduces the built-in types and type constructors of ASN.1, and their type and value notations.

4.1 Simple types

The simple types are the basic building blocks - the atoms - of ASN.1. Each such type is defined directly as a domain of values. All types are ultimately constructed out of the simple types. There are simple types for representing: numerical information (integer, real); finite sets of values (null, Boolean, enumerated); transparent data (bit string, octet string); strings of characters from various character sets; identifiers of "information objects" (object identifier).

Each simple type has a type notation and a value notation. The type notation allows the entire type to be denoted. The value notation allows each particular value of the type to be denoted.

The type notation for all simple types (other than the character strings) begins with one or two keywords, all in upper-case letters. These keywords simple spell out the name in English of the type, and are as follows:

INTEGER
REAL
NULL
BOOLEAN
ENUMERATED
BIT STRING
OCTET STRING
OBJECT IDENTIFIER

The keyword(s) alone constitute valid type notation, except in the case of the enumerated type. For that type, and optionally for the integer and bit string types, the keyword(s) are followed by a list, in braces ({}) of named numbers, each consisting of an identifier followed by a number in round brackets (()). The identifiers introduced in the type notation are used in the value notation.

The type notation for each character string type is a predefined type reference, as for the useful types (see 4.3). These type references again simply spell out the name in English of the type, and are as follows:

NumericString
PrintableString
TeletexString (synonym: **T61String**)
VideotexString
VisibleString (synonym: **ISO646String**)
IA5String
GraphicString
GeneralString

The value notations for the simple types are rather diverse, corresponding to the diversity of the domains of values which they include.

Subtypes of the simple types can be defined by further constraining the values which are included. Several kinds of constraint can be specified, depending on the parent type. All parent types allow for the single value and contained subtype possibilities, and this is not generally restated below. However, specific parent types also allow other possibilities. For example, the numerical types have an order defined on their values, so a subtype can also be defined as a range of values of the parent type.

4.1.1   Integer

The **integer type** is used to represent numerical information, where the numbers involved are all whole numbers (positive or negative). Integers were used in the weather report example above to represent several numerical quantities. (In those examples, the desired precision was inherent in the measurement units chosen, so that whole numbers were appropriate). In addition, the weather reporting example used integer values to identify the various weather stations. This corresponds to the common practice of "numbering" various instances of things, whether it be branches of a chain store or copies of a limited edition print.

The integer type closely corresponds to the mathematical set Z, including as values all of the positive whole numbers:

1, 2, 3, 4, 5, ...

the negative whole numbers:

..., -5, -4, -3, -2, -1

and zero:

0

There is no upper or lower bound on the values, although subtypes of the integer type can of course be defined which do have such bounds. If in some application the values actually envisaged are constrained by some practical consideration, then it is strongly recommended that an appropriate subtype of the integer type be used.

The basic type notation for the integer type is, as mentioned above, simply the keyword **INTEGER**. Optionally, this can be followed by a collection of identifiers for various of the values. For example:

```
BingoNumbers ::= INTEGER
    {
            kellysEye(1), meAndYou(2), youAndMe(3),
            knockAtTheDoor(4), godsInHeaven(7),
            cockAndHen(10), legsEleven(11),
            unluckyForSome(13),
            ... ,
            clicketyClick (66), twoFatLadies(88),
            topOfTheHouse (100)
    }
```

Assigning identifiers in this way can be seen as defining a new type which is like integer, except that it is enriched by a number of built-in names for some **distinguished values**. These names are similar to value references, but are built into the definition of the type.

The numbers corresponding to the identifiers need not form a contiguous range of integers, and they need not appear in the list in any particular order. A particular identifier can only appear once in the list however, and the same is true of the numbers. A popular misconception is that defining names for some integers actually limits the domain of values to just the distinguished values. In fact, no subtyping is implied - the new type still includes all of the integer values, including those which do not have identifiers. (This means that the above example needs to be subtyped, if, as is likely, only the values **1** to **100** (inclusive) are to be allowed).

Many early examples of the use of ASN.1 frequently did use integers for identifying the members of some small finite set of (non-numerical) possibilities, such as:

```
RainbowColour ::= INTEGER
    {
            red(0), orange(1), yellow(2), green(3),
            blue(4), indigo(5), violet(6)
    }
```

ASN.1 now includes the enumerated types (see 4.1.5) for precisely this purpose, so integers should no longer be used in this way.

The notation for integer values is simply the normal decimal notation for numbers. In addition, if distinguished values have been identified, then the identifiers can be used, each denoting the integer value to which it was assigned.

For example, the following are permissible values of **INTEGER**:

```
0
17
22402200
4003383263507000000000
80801742479451287588645990496171075700575436800000000
-143
```

while the following are valid values of the **temperature** component of a **WeatherReport**:

```
-43
0
8
44
```

and:

```
clicketyClick
3
legsEleven
11
60
```

are possible values of **BingoNumbers**. Note that even a distinguished integer value, such as **11** here, can still be written down in its numeric form.

Strictly speaking, although probably not intended, all of the **INTEGER** values are valid as values of **BingoNumbers** because the latter did not involve any subtyping.

Several subtyping constructs are available for integers. Besides single values and contained subtypes, which are valid for all types, value ranges can also be used for integer types because an ordering is defined on the values.

The value range notation involves specifying the lower and upper bounds of the range, separated by "..". Thus we could, and should, have defined **BingoNumbers** thus:

```
BingoNumbers ::= INTEGER
    {
        ...
    }
    (1..100)
```

or even thus:

```
BingoNumbers ::= INTEGER
    {
        ...
    }
    (kellysEye..topOfTheHouse)
```

The lower bound is followed, and the upper bound preceded, by "<" if it is to be excluded from the value set. Sometimes there will not actually be a bound in some direction, the range extending as far as the parent type allows. In that case **MIN** or **MAX** can be used instead of a value for the lower or upper bound respectively.

Thus, for example:

```
Positive ::= INTEGER (0<..MAX)
```

The type **Positive** includes all integer values greater than zero.

This ability to subtype integers allows the designer to express pragmatic constraints on the size of the integers allowed in some situation. For example, the designer may determine that 4-byte integers are adequate for some application, define:

```
LongInt ::= INTEGER (-2147483648..2147483647)
```

and then use **LongInt** everywhere instead of **INTEGER**.

The following are further examples of valid subtypes of **INTEGER**:

```
Temperature ::= INTEGER (-100..60)
Negative ::= INTEGER (MIN..<0)
Zero ::= INTEGER (0)
NonZero ::= INTEGER
    (INCLUDES Negative | INCLUDES Positive)
KnownMersennePrimePowers ::= INTEGER
    (2 | 3 | 5 | 7 | 13 | 17 | 19 | 31 | 61 | 89 | 107 | 127 |
    521 | 607 | 1279 | 2203 | 2281 | 3217 | 4253 | 4423 |
    9689 | 9941 | 11213 | 19937 | 21701 | 23209 |
    44497 | 86243 | 132049 | 216091)
```

and the following of **BingoNumbers**:

```
MyNumbers ::= BingoNumbers
    (legsEleven | unluckyForSome | allTheTwos | 25 |
    allTheSteps | allTheBeans | 67 | 81 | 93)
```

4.1.2 Real

In the first version of ASN.1, the only data type provided for numerical information was the integer type. There is now, in addition, the **real type**, which is used for approximating real numbers by rational numbers. It corresponds to the floating point types found in many programming languages.

The values of the real type are those numbers expressible as:

$$M \times B^E$$

where M is the **mantissa**, and is any integer; B is the **base**, and is 2 or 10; and E is the **exponent**, and is any integer. In addition to these values, the type also includes the special values 0 and $\pm\infty$.

The type notation for the real type is simply the keyword **REAL**.

The value notation provides for the values expressed in terms of M, B, and E to be written down as:

{ M , B , E }

For example, the value of the base of natural logarithms, e, to 24 decimal places can be written as:

```
e REAL ::=  {271828182845904523536Q287, 10, -24}
```

and the Avogadro constant N_A as:

```
nA REAL ::=  {60221367, 10, 16}
```

Special notations are provided for the values of zero, plus-infinity, and minus infinity, as follows:

```
0
PLUS-INFINITY
MINUS-INFINITY
```

The special notation **0** must always be used to represent zero, instead of the full form.

The subtyping possibilities for real are the same as those for integer. The ordering relation defined for real is such that **PLUS-INFINITY** is greater than all other values, while **MINUS-INFINITY** is less than all other values. The following are thus equivalent subtypes of real:

```
PositiveReal1 ::=  REAL (0<..MAX)
PositiveReal2 ::=  REAL (0<..PLUS-INFINITY)
```

and in both cases include the special value **PLUS-INFINITY**.

At present there is no subtyping possibility to limit the precision of a real number, although this is a possible future extension.

4.1.3   Null

The **null type** is somewhat of a curiosity item in ASN.1. Prior to subtyping, it was the only type with just one value. It also provides the only instance in ASN.1 where the same notation, **NULL**, serves to denote both a type and a value (the single value of the type).

It might be thought that, since the information-bearing capacity of a type is related to the number of distinct values, the null type is useless, because, having only one value, it is incapable of conveying any distinction. However, it proves to be useful in a small number of contexts: where a type must be provided but no information needs to be conveyed; when it is necessary to, in effect, enrich the domain of some other type with the "absent" value.

For example, the following type:

```
OptionalInteger ::=  CHOICE{INTEGER, NULL}
```

can be used if an integer value is to be sent when one is available, but sometimes none is available.[11]

In fact ASN.1 provides another way for the designer to indicate that no value of some type may be available. This other approach, the ability to declare components of sets and sequences optional, has some advantages over the use of **NULL**, and this has led to the latter being used only very rarely.

4.1.4 Boolean

The **Boolean type** is used to logical information, information which takes one of the two values true and false.

The type notation is the keyword **BOOLEAN**, the value notation the keywords **TRUE** and **FALSE**.

For example, the following type:

```
StationOperational ::= BOOLEAN
```

could be used to indicate whether some weather station is operational (**TRUE**) or not (**FALSE**).

Where a collection of two-state "variables" occurs, it will frequently be much more efficient to use the bit string type (see 4.1.6) than to make extensive use of Booleans.

4.1.5 Enumerated

The **enumerated types** allow for the modelling of information which takes one of a predefined handful of values. There is not really *an* enumerated type like there is a Boolean type. Instead, users can define their own enumerated types, such as:

```
DaysOfTheWeek ::= ENUMERATED
    {
        sunday(0), monday(1), tuesday(2),
        wednesday(3), thursday(4), friday(5),
        saturday(6)
    }
```

and

```
Priority ::= ENUMERATED {low(-1), medium(0), high(1)}
```

Although the notation is similar to the notation for integers with distinguished values, there are some important differences, besides the use of the keyword **ENUMERATED**.

• the type so defined is restricted to those values which are named;

---

[11]   The "**CHOICE{}**" construct used here provides a capability similar to the union types found in some programming languages, and will be described fully later.

- there is no numerical significance to the numbers involved; they are merely there to provide distinct representations for the various values;
- in particular, there is no ordering relation defined;
- only the identifiers, not the numbers, are used in the value notation.

The value notation possibilities for a particular enumerated type are thus simply those identifiers defined in the type notation. Thus **friday** is a valid value of **DaysOfTheWeek** (which has precisely seven valid values) and **medium** is one of the three valid values of **Priority**.

It would clearly have been possible for the designers of ASN.1 to have omitted the numbers from the notation, so that the user would write something like:

Priority ::= ENUMERATED {low, medium, high}

and the numbers would be implicit, for example, successive numbers from 1 being assigned to successive identifiers. At first glance this would appear to be more "user-friendly". However, the problem with this approach, and the reason it was not adopted, is that it would be more difficult to preserve backwards compatibility in the face of changes. With the numbers explicit, changes can be made simply by adding new items at any appropriate place in the list, ensuring only that the assigned numbers are distinct from those already used.

4.1.6 Bit string

The **bit string type** can be used to model information which is made up of ordered sequences of bits (binary digits). Such a sequence can be of arbitrary length (including zero). The information being modelled may have been produced by some pre-defined coding device or method, for example:

```
FacsimileInformation ::= BIT STRING
Ciphertext ::= BIT STRING
```

Since a bit has the information-bearing capacity of a Boolean, a bit string can also be used to model a collection of two-state values. Doing so is likely to be more compact than the appropriate constructed type (such as **SEQUENCE OF BOOLEAN**). In support of this capability, it is possible to give identifiers to some of the bits. This uses the same notation as for naming distinguished integer values.

Thus:

```
MTControllerStatus ::= BIT STRING
    {
        errorFlag(0), tapeRewinding(1),
        beginningOfTape(2), illegalCommand(3),
        parityError(4), endOfFile(5), endOfTape(6),
        readCompareError(7),
        recordLengthIncorrect(8),dataRequestLate(9),
        badTape(10), tapeFlagOrJobDone(11)
    }
```

The major difference is that the identifiers here do not denote entire values as they do in the case of integers, but simply bit positions.

The first bit in the string has the number 0, and the numbering then increases monotonically, so that if there are n bits in the string, the final bit, also called the **trailing bit**, is bit n-1. This bit numbering is concerned with the (abstract) data values, and does not necessarily bear any relationship to any bit numbering provided by storage or communications media. What relationship there is is entirely the business of the applicable encoding rules.

A popular convention with bit strings, recognised by ASN.1, but unfortunately not fully supported by the notation, is to regard the presence or absence of trailing zero bits as insignificant. Where this convention is in force for a particular bit string, then any value can have trailing zero bits added or removed without changing the meaning. This convention is useful in conjunction with the naming of distinguished bits. What it means is that in a new version of a protocol, names and meanings can be ascribed to new, higher-numbered bits, and, provided that their zero value is used to denote the *status quo*, a backwards-compatible upgrade can be achieved. That is because, albeit unwittingly, implementations of the old version actually generate valid messages under the new.

The value notation for bit strings allows for three different forms, binary, hexadecimal, and identifier-based. The first two involve the direct expression of the value, in one case using binary and in the other using hexadecimal. In each case, the leftmost digit in the value notation defines the lowest-numbered bit or bits. With hexadecimal, each digit describes four consecutive bits, the lowest numbered being the most signficant. The identifier-based form, available only when identifiers have been assigned to some of the bits, involves listing those assigned to the '1' bits (and omitting the '0' bits). Thus:

```
mask BIT STRING ::= '001110111011'B
hexMask BIT STRING ::= '3BB'H
parity MTControllerStatus ::= {errorFlag, parityError}
```

The hexadecimal form is only available when the value is a multiple of four bits in length, or when trailing zero bits are not significant.

The identifier-based method is also only available where trailing zero bits are not significant. In these cases, the value notation describes, not a single value, but a whole family of values which differ only in the number of trailing zero bits.

Besides the single value and contained subtype forms, bit strings can also be subtyped by means of size ranges.

A size range value set includes all of the values whose size, measured in the appropriate units (bits in this case), is within the designated range. The notation is the keyword **SIZE**, followed by some subtype specification which would be suitable for **INTEGER (0..MAX)**.

Thus for example:

```
ShortString ::= BIT STRING (SIZE (0..31))
```

denotes a bit string whose length in bits is in the range **0** to **31** inclusive. Notice the nested parentheses which are due to one subtype specification being found inside another.

Because the general case is that any subtyping construct which would be valid for **INTEGER(0..MAX)** can go in the inner brackets, the following are also permitted (though perhaps a little unlikely!):

```
Odds ::= BIT STRING (SIZE(1 | 3 | 5 | 7 | 9 | 11))
EvenOdder ::= BIT STRING (SIZE(INCLUDES Evens))
Evens ::= INTEGER (2 | 4 | 6 | 8 | 10)
```

4.1.7   Octet string

The **octet string type** can be used to model information which is made up of ordered sequences of octets (8-bit bytes). Such a sequence can be of arbitrary length (including zero). The information being modelled may have been pre-coded by some means, or its coding is may not be relevant at this level of concern,[12] for example:

```
StoreDump ::= OCTET STRING
BinaryFileContents ::= OCTET STRING
```

Unlike the bit string type, no notational support is provided for naming or dealing with particular octets in the octet string.

Two forms of notation are provided for octet string values; binary and hexadecimal, as for bit strings. With both forms, the minimum number of zero digits are considered to be appended so that an integral number of octets results.

With the binary form, each successive group of eight binary digits forms a successive octet, with the leftmost bit in each group being the

---

[12]   There are other methods, notably **ANY** and **EXTERNAL** (and of course **BIT STRING**) for incorporating information which is not fully known at this level of description. More on this later.

most significant. With the hexadecimal form, each successive pair of hexadecimal digits forms a successive octet, with the first digit in the pair being the more significant.

Thus, the following octet string values are all the same:

```
os1  OCTET STRING ::=    '000010101110000111'B
os2  OCTET STRING ::=    '000010101110000111000000'B
os3  OCTET STRING ::=    '0AE1C'H
os3  OCTET STRING ::=    '0AE1C0'H
```

The forms of subtyping allowed for octet strings are the same as for bit strings except that, with a size range, the size is measured in octets. Thus:

```
AtLeastOneOctet ::= OCTET STRING (SIZE (1..MAX))
```

defines a octet string which can be of any length except zero, while:

```
RestrictedLength ::= OCTET STRING (SIZE (0..255))
```

restricts the maximum length of the octet string to 255 octets.

4.1.8 Character strings

The **character string types** can be used to model textual information, information composed of ordered sequences of characters. There are eight character string types in ASN.1, two of them with alternative names. Each has an associated character set from which all characters in the string must be drawn.

The characters included in the various types are as follows:

NumericString	0 - 9 and space
PrintableString	a - z A - Z 0 - 9 ' " ( ) + , - . / : = ? and space
TeletexString **(T61String)**	character set as defined by CCITT Recommendation T.61
VideotexString	character sets as defined by CCITT Recommendations T.100, T.101
VisibleString **(ISO646String)**	visible characters of IA5 (international version of ASCII) plus space
IA5String	all characters of IA5
GraphicString	all registered[13] graphic characters plus space
GeneralString	all registered graphic and control characters plus space and delete

---

[13]   Registers are maintained, on behalf of ISO, of graphic and control character sets.

There is presently a good deal of confusion in the area of character
string types. One short-term problem was caused by ASN.1 quoting
the register numbers to be used in **TeletexString**. When CCITT
Recommendation T.61 was updated in 1988 to add support for,
among others, the Hebrew and Greek character sets, the
corresponding update was not made in ASN.1. This is now being
fixed.

More serious, perhaps, is the question of what character set type
to use in a particular application. Some international standards use
TeletexString to convey text, while others use **GraphicString**. The
latter is more flexible, but it is also more unpredictable: a received
value could have virtually anything in it, without any outward
identification of what is actually there. This makes it very difficult to
implement.

In retrospect, it would have been far better had ASN.1 had a
single character string type with flexible ways of defining subsets of
the characters involved. This may yet come to pass, thanks to the
emergence, from the character set standardisation community, of a
new standard, ISO 10646 (still under development), which
encompasses the characters used in the world's written languages as
well as specialised scripts used in linguistics and mathematics.
These developments are described further in 9.3.

The notation for a character string value is simply the printed
form of the string between double quotes ("""). A double quote in the
string itself is represented by a pair of double quotes.

For example, the following are permitted values:

```
myExtension NumericString ::= "5690"
longPlaceName PrintableString ::= "Coignafeuinternich"
mostAccents TeletexString ::= "újjáépítésére"
acropolis GraphicString ::= "ακροπολισ"
quotableQuote PrintableString ::= "double quote is """""""
```

There are some significant drawbacks to this notation. There is no
standard way of continuing a string onto a different line, as can be
done, for example, in C by ending a line with backslash. (While lines
are not bounded in length in ASN.1, they are on all known print
media!). There is no way of showing the inclusion of control
characters, or of graphic characters which cannot be rendered on the
medium being defined. There is no way of reliably distinguishing
between characters whose glyphs are similar in appearance, such as
LATIN CAPITAL LETTER H and CYRILLIC CAPITAL LETTER EN.

These problems are expected to be overcome by the enhancement
work in progress.

Several subtyping constructs are available for character strings. They are single value and contained subtype, which are valid for all types, together with size range and permitted alphabet.

In a size range value set, the unit of measure is the character. Thus, for example:

```
SociallnsuranceNumber ::= NumericString (SIZE(9))
```

is a subtype of **NumericString** all of whose values are exactly nine characters in length.

A permitted alphabet value set allows the string to be constrained as regards the characters it may contain. This is accomplished by following the keyword **FROM** by a valid subtype specification for the single character string of the same type. This subtype specification is effectively limited to using single value and contained subtypes.

Thus, for example:

```
Morse ::= PrintableString (FROM ("." | "-" | " "))

ClassicalLatinWord ::= PrintableString (FROM
    ("A" | "B" | "C" | "D" | "E" | "F" | "G" | "H" | "I" | "K" | "L" | "M" |
     "N" | "O" | "P" | "Q" | "R" | "S" | "T" | "U" | "X" | "Y" | "Z"))
```

where each denotes a printable string whose characters include only those listed.

If both the size and the permitted characters in the string are to be constrained, then a two-stage subtype will normally be required. For example, if, as is likely, **SociallnsuranceNumbers** are not allowed to contain spaces, then the definition:

```
SociallnsuranceNumber ::= NumericString
    (SIZE (9))
    (FROM ("0" | "1" | "2" | "3" | "4" | "5" | "6" | "7" | "8" | "9")
```

is required. The following is similar in appearance, but has a very different effect:

```
AntiSociallnsuranceNumber ::= NumericString
    (SIZE (9)
    | FROM ("0" | "1" | "2" | "3" | "4" | "5" | "6" | "7" | "8" | "9")
```

The values of this type are *either* 9 characters in length *or* contain no spaces (or both). Thus, "1 3 5 7 9" and "13579" are valid values.

4.1.9   Object identifier

The **object identifier type**, while *technically* a simple type, is actually far from it. The values of the type correspond to the nodes of the **object identifier tree** (OIT), a tree set up to allow the unambiguous naming of **information objects**.

Many general-purpose application protocols introduce the concept of some kind of information object, and define the characteristics that such objects have in general, for example the operations that can be carried out upon them. They then leave it to others to design the particular information objects to be used in some situation. For instance, a distributed file service specification may introduce the *notions* of file type and file attribute, but leave it to others to design particular file types (for example the "Whizzo Spreadsheet" file format) or attributes.

A recurring problem with such open-ended applications is the identification of the specific information object(s) involved in some instance of communication. The operation to open a file, for example, may be defined to return an indication of the file type. The purpose of this is for the process reading the file to be able to know how to interpret the file contents (or, at a minimum, to find out that it does not know how). The question, then, is "what's the form of that identifier?".

Some of the most obvious answers turn out not to work very well, or indeed at all.

Take integers, for example, an approach which has been used in the past. The problem here is that one either has to have a central registration authority (Whizzo Corporation is allocated numbers 76000-76999 for its use) or the potential for clashes and hence ambiguity (Whizzo Corp. and Snafu, Inc. independently think that no-one else would dream of allocating the number 999).

Character strings are fine for human readability, but they have the same problems as integers: you either have a central registration authority or risk clashes.

The solution actually adopted involves the design of a hierarchical system of registration authorities based around the OIT. Every organisation who wishes to allocate object identifiers; that is, every organisation who wishes to design or register one or more information objects, gets itself a node in the tree. Particular designs are placed at the leaves (generally) of this tree, subordinate to the organisation which is registering them. Each node of the tree provides unique (non-negative) integers for each of its subordinates. It is then possible to uniquely identify any node as a sequence of integers. The upper reaches of the OIT are shown in Appendix D.

For example, the jointly-designed ISO/CCITT directory telephone number attribute is uniquely and unambiguously identified by the sequence of four integers 2, 5, 4, and 20. Actually it is also distinguishable from every other information object, not just from other attribute types. At first sight this seems like overkill but it actually has some significant advantages, not least of which is that a single tree suffices for every kind of information object, even kinds that have not been invented yet. In any case the supply of object identifiers is of course inexhaustible, so nothing is lost.

Among the kinds of information object in OSI standardisation which are presently identified by this means are:

- modules, application contexts, abstract syntaxes, transfer syntaxes (or encoding rules), application entity types (all applications)
- document types, constraint sets (FTAM);
- attribute types, attribute syntaxes, attribute sets, object classes, algorithms (X.500 Directory);
- content types, encoded information types, attribute types, token types, secure agent types, security categories, security policies, auto-action-types, extended body-part types, heading extensions (X.400 MHS);
- operations, errors (ROS).

The object identifier type is employed whenever it is necessary to convey one of these identifiers. The type notation is simply the keywords **OBJECT IDENTIFIER**. Thus:

```
FileType ::= OBJECT IDENTIFIER
AttributeType ::= OBJECT IDENTIFIER
Module ::= OBJECT IDENTIFIER
```

The value notation is rather more complicated. The aim in every case is to specify the sequence of non-negative integers constituting the object identifier value. However, there are a number of ways that the successive integers can be expressed.

The simplest form to describe (though not necessarily to use) simply involves a list of numbers in braces (*not* separated by commas) thus:

```
telephoneNumber AttributeType ::= {2 5 4 20}
weatherReporting Module ::= {2 6 6 247 1}
```

The first of these is a sequence of four numbers, the second of five numbers.

Various symbolic options are also provided.

The initial item in the braces can be a value reference assigned to some other object identifier value. That value identifies some starting point in the OIT and the sequence of numbers which follow are then relative to that point.

For the first several arcs from the root, various predefined symbolic names are provided and can be used instead of the equivalent numbers. Thus, there are the following equivalences:

```
    {0}      ≡    {ccitt}
    {1}      ≡    {iso}
    {2}      ≡    {joint-iso-ccitt}
    {0 0}    ≡    {ccitt recommendation}
    {0 0 1}  ≡    {ccitt recommendation a}
      ...            ...
```

```
{0 0 26}  ≡   {ccitt recommendation z}
{0 1}     ≡   {ccitt question}
{0 2}     ≡   {ccitt administration}
{0 3}     ≡   {ccitt network-operator}
{1 0}     ≡   {iso standard}
{1 1}     ≡   {iso registration-authority}
{1 2}     ≡   {iso member-body}
{1 3}     ≡   {iso identified-organization}
```

For subsequent numbers, a symbolic name (identifier) can be supplied in addition to the number - in this case the number is placed in round brackets (()).

Finally, any number can be expressed by a value reference which has been assigned to a (non-negative) integer value.

As a result of these various possibilities, we see some more complex forms of object identifier:

```
directory OBJECT IDENTIFIER ::= {joint-iso-ccitt ds(5)}
attributeType OBJECT IDENTIFIER ::=
                        {directory attributeTypes(4)}
telephoneNumber OBJECT IDENTIFIER ::=
                        {attributeType 20}
```

The first of these is equivalent to {2 5}, the second to {2 5 4}, and the third to {2 5 4 20}.

The only forms of subtyping applicable to object identifiers are single value and contained subtype.

4.2   Structured types

The structured types of ASN.1 are defined in terms of other types, their **components**. The values of structured types are generally derived from values of the component types. The component types may themselves be structured, and this can occur to the depth appropriate to the needs of the application.

The number of possible structured types is unbounded, although there are only a small number of methods by which they can be constructed. There are types whose values are collections of component values, either of different types (set, sequence) or of a single type (set-of, sequence-of). There are types whose values are chosen from those of a number of component types (choice), and a type (any) whose values are those of all other types. There are (tagged) types, each of which is isomorphic to some other type.

Subtypes of the structured types can be defined by further constraining the values which are included. Several kinds of constraint can be specified, depending on the parent type. Subtypes of many structured types can be defined by means of subtyping their components.

The type notation for all structured types (except the tagged types) begins with one or two keywords, all in upper-case letters, and which spell out, in English, the name of the type construction method. They are as follows:

SET
SEQUENCE
SET OF
SEQUENCE OF
CHOICE
ANY

The type notation for the tagged types begins with a *tag*, displayed in square brackets ([ ]).

The value notations for the structured types are generally defined in terms of the value notation for their components.

4.2.1 Set

A **set type** is defined in terms of a collection of component types, all distinct. Each value of a set type contains a value of each of the component types. Thus, a set type can be used to model an information record, where each of the components models some aspect (field) of it.

The type notation allows the component types to be listed, in arbitrary order. Each component type is preceded by an identifier, which can be regarded as the name of the component.

For example:

```
TypA ::= SET
{
     p    BOOLEAN,
     q    INTEGER,
     r    BIT STRING
}
```

Each value of **TypA** must contain one value of component **p** (a **BOOLEAN** value), one of **q** (an **INTEGER** value), and one of **r** (a **BIT STRING** value). The component values appear in no particular order.

The value notation for a set type consists of the list of component values (in braces and separated by commas).

Among the possible values is the following:

```
valA TypA ::=
{
     p     TRUE,
     r     '83F'H,
     q     -7
}
```

Notice that the component values appear here in a different order to that in which the component types appeared in the type notation. This is quite permissible, and has no significance.

Each component value is preceded by its identifier. Because the order is arbitrary, the identifiers are needed to ensure unambiguous value notation. Consider the following example, in which the identifiers are omitted:

```
TypB ::= SET
{
    BIT STRING,
    OCTET STRING
}
valB TypB ::=
{
    '0110'H,
    '0111'H
}
```

In **valB**, is the value **'0110'H** the **BIT STRING** value, or the **OCTET STRING** value? There is, of course, no way to tell, so the value notation is ambiguous.

ASN.1 does actually allow the identifiers to be omitted, and warns that this may lead to ambiguous value notation. This is somewhat unsatisfactory, and likely arose from the view that notation for values was not always needed, abstract syntaxes being defined primarily in terms of types. However this misses the point that the author of the type notation does not always know whether or not values will need to be specified. Furthermore, if the identifiers are chosen carefully, they can provide useful insight to the reader as to the purpose of the various components. They also allow the components to be discussed or specified further in text. In practice, therefore, there is no real justification for omitting the identifiers, and they should always be provided.

It was stated above that the various component types of a set type must be "distinct", and in the examples above, the types of the components clearly are. However, this constraint would seem to make the set types useless for most practical purposes, because there is no reason to expect that components, each independently chosen to model some particular aspect of a complex type, should just happen to be distinct.

Step forward please... the tagged types. Corresponding to every type is a family of possible tagged types, each having the same information-bearing capacity as the original type, but distinct from it. One of the main purposes of the tagged types is to allow the various components of set types (and choice types, see 4.2.5) to be made distinct.

The simplest, and most useful, type notation for a tagged type is obtained by preceding the original type notation by a number in square brackets. Since two tagged types are distinct whenever the numbers are different, then the distinctness requirements of set types can be satisfied by making all of the components tagged types with different numbers.

Thus, the following is a well-formed set type:

```
TypC ::= SET
{
    t     [0]   INTEGER,
    u     [1]   INTEGER,
    v     [2]   BOOLEAN
}
```

Tagging does not affect the value notation. Thus an example value of this type is as follows:

```
valC TypC ::= { t -5, v TRUE, u 0}
```

Notice that the **v** component of **TypC** is tagged even though it did not really need to be (**BOOLEAN**s are inherently distinct from **INTEGER**s). It is however a fairly common discipline to tag all members of a set type rather than just those that need it. This avoids the effort of checking whether tagging is strictly needed. Such checking may be tedious, particularly where some of the components are defined types, possibly even imported from other modules.

The tagged types are more fully described in in 4.2.7 below.

One area where set types are frequently used is in forming the overall structure of protocol data units (PDUs). Frequently such a PDU is made up of a number of fields or parameters which are the components of the set.

For example:

```
RejectTPDU ::= SET
{
    destRef      [0]   Reference,
    yr-tu-nr     [1]   TPDUnumber,
    credit       [2]   Credit
}
```

PDUs are frequently defined with fields that need not always be present. For example, in the OSI Transport Protocol,[14] many of the messages (TPDUs) have a "variable part", containing such optional fields. This is actually a fairly common situation, and is catered for in ASN.1 by the **OPTIONAL** keyword, which can be placed after the type of an omittable component.

---

[14]   The OSI Transport Protocol does not actually make use of ASN.1, and in fact predates it. However, there is actually no real reason why ASN.1 should not be used for defining such "low-level" protocols.

As an example:

```
ExpeditedDataAcknowledgement ::= SET
{
    destRef        [0]  Reference,
    yr-tu-nr       [1]  TPDUnumber,
    checkSum       [2]  CheckSum OPTIONAL
}
```

Here, the **checkSum** component is not always present in this TPDU. The circumstances and significance of its actual omission from a particular message must be specified by the designer. In this respect, "absence" can be regarded as similar to an extra value of that component. The notation for a value of the set type in which a certain component is absent, simply omits any mention of that component, as follows:

```
{
    destRef        ...,
    yr-tu-nr       ...
}
```

One reason for making a field of a protocol message optional is to allow it to be omitted when it assumes a particular value, perhaps that which occurs most frequently. By this means, the explicit sending of that value can be avoided. Support is provided in ASN.1 for the designation of such a default value for a component.

For example:

```
DataAcknowledgementTPDU ::= SET
{
    destRef        [0]  Reference,
    yr-tu-nr       [1]  TPDUnumber,
    checkSum       [2]  CheckSum OPTIONAL,
    subSeqNr       [3]  SubSequenceNumber DEFAULT 0,
    flowCntrlCnf   [4]  FlowControlConfirmation OPTIONAL
}
```

Here the **subSeqNr** component is effectively always present; however the default value, **0**, can be represented implicitly by the omission of the component. The default value can still be represented explicitly, and the two possibilities result in the same overall value.

It should be noted that declaring a component to be optional and declaring a default for it are in general very different (they are also mutually exclusive). While the former case allows for the complete omission of the component value, the latter is saying that in effect the component is always present, because even its omission is pressed into service to represent a specific value.

Normally, when one set type appears in the definition of another, it forms just one component of the latter, and the nested structure is preserved. It is possible however, to include the components of one set type as direct components of another. This is accomplished by means of the **COMPONENTS OF** construct.

For example:

```
TypD ::= SET
{
    f     [1]  INTEGER OPTIONAL,
    g     [2]  BOOLEAN,
    h     [3]  BIT STRING,
}
TypE ::= SET
{
    j     REAL,
    k     OCTET STRING OPTIONAL,
    COMPONENTS OF TypD
}
```

Here **TypE** is defined to have components **f**, **g**, and **h**, as defined in **TypD**, as well as **j** and **k**.

The **COMPONENTS OF** construct is not a component itself, and consequently does not have an identifier. As in this example, the type following the **OF** must itself be a set type.

This construct is not much used, because normally, when including a set type within another, one actually wants the former to be a single component of the latter. Where it could be useful is in defining, in one place, components common to several set types.

There are some drawbacks with the construct, however. Firstly, by including the components of another set type directly, the problem of ensuring distinctness of types arises again. This time the approach of tagging the components in every set type fails to help, and indeed conflicts, with the solution of this problem. Secondly, one must take care not to introduce recursion or mutual dependencies of set types.

The following is illegal (but sometimes tricky to detect):

```
TypF ::= SET
{
    p   INTEGER,
    COMPONENTS OF TypG
}

TypG ::= SET
{
    q   REAL,
    COMPONENTS OF TypF
}
```

The most useful subtyping mechanism for set types is **inner subtyping**. Here, a subtype of a set type is defined by subtyping some or all of the component types and/or by imposing constraints over the presence or absence of optional components.

Each inner subtyping construct for a set type begins with the keywords **WITH COMPONENTS**, and includes a list of constraints, each concerning one of the components of the set type. The constraint begins with the identifier of the component[15] and continues with either a suitable subtype specification for that component, or a presence constraint (denoted by one of the keywords **ABSENT, PRESENT, OPTIONAL**) or both, or neither.

There are two alternative styles of inner subtyping, full specification and partial specification. They differ mainly in the effect of not providing a constraint for some of the components.

In a full specification, wherein the list of constraints is included in braces, omission is only permitted for optional (and default) components. The omission of an optional component implies a presence constraint of **ABSENT**, so that values of that component are not included in any values of the subtype. Further, in a full specification, an optional component for which no presence constraint is provided is deemed to be **PRESENT**.[16]

In a partial specification, wherein the list of constraints has a special opening bracket ("{...,"), any component for which no constraint is provided is unchanged relative to the parent type.[17]

As an example of inner subtyping, consider the type **Expedited-DataAcknowledgement** which is defined above as follows:

```
ExpeditedDataAcknowledgement ::= SET
{
        destRef        [0]   Reference,
        yr-tu-nr       [1]   TPDUnumber,
        checkSum       [2]   CheckSum OPTIONAL
}
```

We will assume the following definition:

```
TPDUnumber ::= INTEGER (0..2147483647)
```

---

15 thus providing further rationale, if any were needed, for always assigning identifiers to the components of a set type.

16 This is slightly counter-intuitive, as one might expect that the "default" would be continued optionality. The reason derives from an attempt to mimic the set value notation, in which the presence or absence of a value of an optional component is denoted simply by its presence or absence in the list.

17 In the special opening bracket, the ellipsis ("...") really does appear in the notation, and is not simply being used by this author as an abbreviation.

We might wish to define a type whose values are a subset of the values of **ExpeditedDataAcknowledgement**, namely those for which the **yr-tu-nr** component is in the range **0** to **127**, and the **checkSum** component absent. This subtype can be defined as either (using full specification):

```
NormalEA ::= ExpeditedDataAcknowledgement
    (
        WITH COMPONENTS
            {
                destRef,
                yr-tu-nr (0..127)
            }
    )
```

or equivalently (using partial specification) as:

```
NormalEA ::= ExpeditedDataAcknowledgement
    (
        WITH COMPONENTS
            {...,
                yr-tu-nr (0..127),
                checkSum ABSENT
            }
    )
```

We can also define another subtype in which the full range of **TPDUnumbers** is allowed, but in which the **checkSum** must be present. Again, there are two possibilities, depending on whether full or partial specification is employed.

With full specification, the following is used:

```
ExtendedEA ::= ExpeditedDataAcknowledgment
    (
        WITH COMPONENTS
            {destRef, yr-tu-nr, checkSum}
    )
```

while with partial specification:

```
ExtendedEA ::= ExpeditedDataAcknowledgement
    (WITH COMPONENTS {..., checkSum PRESENT})
```

Since the single value and contained subtype constructs are also available, then we can define:

```
EA ::= ExpeditedDataAcknowledgement
    (INCLUDES NormalEA | INCLUDES ExtendedEA)
```

In this type, either the **checksum** is absent, in which case **yr-tu-nr** must be in the range **0..127**, or the **checksum** is present, in which case there is no additional constraint on **yr-tu-nr**.

As can be seen, the use of inner subtyping allows the definition of two or more types which have significant commonality by defining their common parent and subtyping it. This makes the relationship between the types clear, and encourages this to be maintained if the types evolve. It also suggests and facilitates common support for the types in an implementation.

The choice between full and partial specification is a matter of taste and convenience. For example, if the envisaged subtype is more constrained than the parent type in only a few of the components, then partial specification is probably more appropriate, as it focuses the readers' attention on the differences from the parent type. On the other hand, if all or most of the components are affected, then a full specification is probably clearer.

4.2.2   Sequence

Sequence types are very similar in syntax and application to set types. The major difference is that the order in which the component values appear is fixed, being that in which the component types appear in the definition.

Thus, given:

```
TypH ::= SEQUENCE
{
    r    INTEGER,
    s    BOOLEAN,
    t    INTEGER  OPTIONAL
}
```

the following are valid values:

```
valH1  TypH ::= {r -5, s TRUE, t 0}
valH2  TypH ::= {10, FALSE}
```

while the following is not:

```
invalidVal TypH ::= {t 1, r 2, s TRUE}
```

Sequence types are used in preference to set types when there is some natural order, inherent to the application, in which the components will be generated, or will need to be processed. For example, in the X.400 message transfer system, a message, made up of an "envelope" and "contents", is defined thus:

```
Message ::= SEQUENCE
{
    envelope      MessageTransferEnvelope,
    content       Content
}
```

Message is defined as a sequence type with the components in that order because the application needs to deal with the **envelope** component before the **content** component. Encoding rules can be defined so that the components are conveyed in the appropriate order (the BER have this characteristic), and, depending on the implementation, the receiving application software may have access to earlier components before later ones have actually been transferred.

While an ordering constraint is imposed on sequence (but not set) types, the distinctness constraint which is imposed on set types is relaxed somewhat for sequences. In fact, where a sequence has no optional (or default) components, there is no distinctness constraint at all. Thus:

```
TypJ ::= SEQUENCE {INTEGER, INTEGER, INTEGER}
```

is quite valid. It is also more acceptable under these circumstances to omit the identifiers, as has been done in this example, because the fixed order of appearance of the components eliminates the ambiguity which can arise with set types. (Notwithstanding this, the documentation advantages of naming the components by means of identifiers should not be sacrificed lightly).

Even where a sequence type has some optional (or default) components, it is still not necessary for all of their types to be distinct.[18] The rule is that where one or more consecutive components are optional (or have defaults), their types must be distinct from each other, and from the immediately following mandatory component, if there is one.

As an example, TypH above is legal, despite having two INTEGER components, one optional. That is because there is only one optional component, and it is the last one. On the other hand, the following:

```
InvalidTypH ::= SEQUENCE
{
    t      INTEGER OPTIONAL,
    r      INTEGER,
    s      BOOLEAN
}
```

where t has been made the first, instead of the last, component, is invalid. This is because the optional component t is not distinct from the mandatory component r, which follows it. The reason for this rule is to allow the straightforward analysis of a received value against the definition.

While receiving a value, the receiver does not know which component, within a "run" of optionals, will appear next, as that depends on which, if any, have actually been omitted. If all of the rest of the optionals in that run have been omitted, then the value of the next mandatory component (or perhaps the end of the sequence)

---

[18] This was, however, required by CCITT Recommendation X.409, and by the first ASN.1 standard.

will be encountered. In order properly to associate received values with the correct components, distinctness is required.

Although not stated in the ASN.1 specification, a similar rule is recommended in determining where it might be acceptable to omit the identifiers.

The **COMPONENTS OF** construct is applicable within a sequence type, but, as one might expect, the type to which it refers must also be a sequence type.

The subtyping possibilities for sequence types are the same as for set types, except that the constraints must appear in order. Ambiguities can arise, as with the value notation, if identifiers are omitted and there are optional types. However, ambiguities can also arise even where there are no optional components, if partial specification is employed.

4.2.3   Set-of

A **set-of type** is defined in terms of a single component type, and its values are the unordered collections of values of the component type. A particular component value can appear more than once, and the number of occurrences is significant.[19]

The type notation consists of the keywords **SET OF** followed by the type of the components.

Thus, given a type **Parameter**, the derived type:

```
Parameters ::= SET OF Parameter
```

has as its values all of the unordered collections of **Parameter** values.

Where the component type is the any type (see 4.2.6), the resulting **SET OF ANY** can be abbreviated to **SET**. However, although permitted, this abbreviation should be avoided, because it makes possible some pieces of ASN.1, albeit pathological, which are difficult to analyse, and as a result may be removed from the language.

The notation for a value of a set-of type simply lists the component values, in any order, in braces and separated by commas.

For example:

```
v1 SET OF INTEGER ::= {0,0,-3,1,-3,1,948,-238981,0,-3}
v2 SET OF INTEGER ::= {-238981,-3,-3,-3,0,0,0,1,1,948}
```

The values **v1** and **v2** are the same.

The value which is the empty collection of component values is denoted by empty braces (**{ }**).

Because the order in which the various component values appear is not significant, this type should only be used in contexts where the component values are self-identifying, or do not need to be

---

19   The term **bag** has been employed elsewhere for this concept.

individually identified. This is in contrast to the sequence-of types (4.2.4).

Subtypes of set-of types can be defined using the size range and inner subtyping notations. A size range is specified using the same **SIZE** construct which is available for the various strings, but here the unit of measure is the component value, rather than the bit, octet, or character.

It is important to note that if a subtype specification is placed directly after the notation for a set-of type, then it is considered to form part of the component type. Thus

TypJ ::= SET OF PrintableString (SIZE (5))

is a type whose values are the collections (of any size) of values, each of which is a string of five printable characters.

To limit the size of the set-of, rather than of its components, it is necessary either to use a defined type[20], thus:

TypK ::= SET OF PrintableString
TypL ::= TypK (SIZE (5))

or to use a special notation provided for the purpose:

TypM ::= SET SIZE (5) OF PrintableString

where the size range appears between the **SET** and the **OF**. Notice that here the size range is not in brackets, because it is the only subtyping construct which can appear there, and the general case is not permitted.

Inner subtyping is available for set-of types. Here the value set takes the form of the keywords **WITH COMPONENT** (note the singular) followed by a subtype specification valid for the component type.

Inner subtyping will not generally be used except with a defined type which is a set-of type. This is because:

TypJ ::= SET WITH COMPONENT (SIZE(5)) OF PrintableString

is much clumsier than its more direct definition above. On the other hand, if a defined type such as **TypK** has already been defined, then **TypJ** must be defined:

TypJ ::= TypK (WITH COMPONENT (SIZE(5))

4.2.4 Sequence-of

The **sequence-of types** resemble the set-of types, the main difference being that the order of the component values is significant,

---

[20] This example demonstrates that the use of defined types is not the same as textual substitution.

Thus, a sequence-of type is defined in terms of a single component type, and its values are the ordered collections, i.e. lists, of values of the component type.

The difference between the sequence-of types and the set-of types, namely the significance of the order, is similar to the difference between sequence and set types. However, it is somewhat more important here, as the order can be used to convey information. One way of looking at this is that every component value has an associated positive integer value, its position in the list.

All of the same notational possibilities (type, value, and subtype) are available as for set-of types, except that the keyword **SEQUENCE** is used instead of **SET**.

For example a list of temperature readings could be represented as a value of the following type:

```
Readings ::= SEQUENCE OF Temperature
```

where

```
Temperature ::= INTEGER (-100..60)
```

The position of a temperature reading in the list can be used to represent some quantity, such as time. Thus, with a known starting time T, and time interval t, the values in the list could successively represent the temperatures at times T, $T+t$, $T+2t$, and so on.

For example the following values:

```
nagoya Readings ::=
    {8,9,11,18,23,26,29,32,29,22,17,10}
medicineHat Readings ::=
    {-5,-4,4,15,20,24,29,28,20,15,3,-2}
```

could represent the average daily maximum temperatures in various locations for the months of a certain year, beginning with January. There is no need to convey an explicit indication of the month for each reading, because that can be inferred from the position in the list.

Sequence-of types can be used to represent arrays, with subtyping being used to fix their bounds (or to be precise, their extents). For example, the following data type

```
Arr ::= SEQUENCE SIZE(6) OF
            SEQUENCE SIZE(2) OF INTEGER
```

could be used to represent an array similar to the Pascal declaration:

var arr : array [1..6,1..2] of integer

Note carefully that if a range, like **1..6**, had been used instead of the value **6** in the first size constraint in the definition of **Arr**, then this would not have meant that the bounds were 1 to 6, as in Pascal, but that the array's first dimension varied in extent between **1** and **6**.

An example value of this array is the following:

```
arrVal Arr ::
    {
        {  5,        6},
        { 17,      -30},
        { 20,       20},
        {  0,        1},
        {  0,       -1},
        { -1,       35}
    }
```

4.2.5 Choice

A **choice type** is defined in terms of a collection of component types, its **alternatives**, which must all be distinct. Each value of a component type is a value of just one of the alternatives. The choice types are similar to the union types found in some programming languages.

The type notation begins with the keyword **CHOICE**, which is followed by the list of alternatives in braces and separated by commas. Each alternative can be preceded by an identifier. As with set types, it is suggested that identifiers always be provided, so as to avoid ambiguity in the value and subtype notations.

Distinctness of the alternatives can be ensured, as with set types, by use of tagged types. Again, it is common practice to tag all of the alternatives of a choice, whether or not they actually need it.

For example:

```
TypN ::= CHOICE
    {
        x    [0]   REAL,
        y    [1]   INTEGER,
        z    [2]   NumericString
    }
```

The value notation for a choice type is simply the value of the selected alternative, preceded by the appropriate identifier, if there is one. For example:

```
v1 TypN ::= x {50, 10, -1}
v2 TypN ::= z "5"
```

If a choice type is itself used (untagged) in some context where distinct types are needed, for instance as a component of a set type or an encompassing choice type, then all of the components of the inner choice must be distinct from all of the components of the set or outer choice.

The following is therefore illegal:

```
Illegal ::= CHOICE
    {
        a CHOICE {INTEGER,BOOLEAN},
        b CHOICE {BOOLEAN, NULL}
    }
```

because both alternatives of **a** would need to be distinct from both alternatives of **b**, whereas **BOOLEAN** appears in both.

If **a** and **b** are tagged, however, then it does not matter what *their* components are; distinctness is assured. Thus:

```
Legal ::= CHOICE
    {
        a    [0]  CHOICE {INTEGER,BOOLEAN},
        b    [1]  CHOICE {BOOLEAN, NULL}
    }
```

A choice type is used when the values to be described can be of different types under different circumstances, and where all of the possibilities are known in advance.

For example, the various PDUs of a protocol will be of different types, depending on the information which they include. The overall abstract syntax for that protocol, then, can be described as a choice type where the various PDUs are the alternatives.

Thus:

```
TransportProtocolPDU ::= CHOICE
    {
        connectionRequest    [0]    CR,
        connectionConfirm    [1]    CC,
        disconnectRequest    [2]    DR,
        disconnectConfirm    [3]    DC,
        data                 [4]    DT,
        expeditedData        [5]    ED,
        dataAck              [6]    AK,
        expeditedDataAck     [7]    EA,
        reject               [8]    RJ,
        error                [9]    ER
    }
```

Protocols defined in this way do not need an explicit "PDU type" component, as the distinction between the various PDUs is conveyed by the distinctness of the alternatives, and is achieved by tagging.

Another common use of choice types arises where the same information can be represented in two or more ways in some application. For example, a chemical element may be identified by either its atomic number or symbol, or a country may be identified by either a numerical or alphabetic code. In each case, the type can be described as a choice whose alternatives correspond to the various possibilities.

For example:

```
Element ::= CHOICE
    {
        atomicNumber      INTEGER (1..109),
        symbol            PrintableString (SIZE(1..2))
    }
```

includes the following values:

```
arsenic-S Element ::=      symbol    "As"
nitrogen-S Element ::=     symbol    "N"
hydrogen-N Element ::=     atomicNumber 1
```

It is worthy of note that one approach to extending an ASN.1 type, such as to define a new version of some protocol, is to add new alternatives to an existing choice. Accordingly, if some type is seen as only the first of a possible list of alternatives to represent some information, then it helps to make it a choice type with just one alternative initially.

For example, the definition of **Name** in the first version of the OSI Directory standard (X.500) is as follows:

```
Name ::= CHOICE
    {   -- only one possibility for now --
        RDNSequence
    }
```

As well as being useful to declare future possibilities, this avoids the possibility of optimisations in some encoding rules which would prevent the backwards-compatible addition of new alternatives.

It sometimes arises that not all of the alternatives of a choice are to be allowed in some context. This can be done by means of inner subtyping, as described below, or by means of selection types.

A **selection type** is a type which is restricted to just one of the alternatives of a choice. It is therefore equivalent to the type of the selected alternative, and requires that that alternative has been assigned an identifier. The notation for a selection type is the identifier of the relevant alternative, and the name of the choice type, separated by "<", which can be read as "alternative of".

For example, if in some situation only the **symbol** alternative of **Element** is to be allowed, that can be expressed as follows:

```
SymbolicForm ::= symbol < Element
```

If the selection type notation is used within another choice (or within a set or sequence), then the identifier can be used as the identifier for the resulting component in value or subtype notation.

Thus, given:

```
BothForms ::= SEQUENCE
    {
        atomicNumber < Element,
        symbol < Element
    }
```

the following is a valid value:

```
strontium BothForms ::= {atomicNumber 38, symbol "Sr"}
```

However, it is also possible to provide a new, overriding identifier for such a component, as follows:

```
BothForms ::= SEQUENCE
    {
        numeric      atomicNumber < Element,
        symbolic     symbol < Element
    }
```

whereupon the notation for the above value would have been:

```
strontium BothForms ::= {numeric 38, symbolic "Sr"}
```

A very similar effect to selection types can be achieved by constructing the choice from defined types, whose references could then be used directly if there was a requirement to refer to just one of the alternatives.

To define a choice of some limited number of the alternatives, selection types can be used as follows:

```
Class0PDU ::= CHOICE
    {
        connectionRequest < TransportProtocolPDU,
        connectionConfirm < TransportProtocolPDU,
        disconnectRequest < TransportProtocolPDU,
        data < TransportProtocolPDU,
        error < TransportProtocolPDU
    }
```

However, this is rather indirect, and requires the repetition of the name of the original choice. Better is the use of inner subtyping, as follows:

```
Class0PDU ::= TransportProtocolPDU
    (WITH COMPONENTS {
        connectionRequest,
        connectionConfirm,
        disconnectRequest,
        data,
        error}
    )
```

Inner subtyping can also be used to list the disallowed alternatives explicitly if that is more useful or concise:

```
Class4PDU ::= TransportProtocolPDU
    (WITH COMPONENTS{..., reject ABSENT})
```

Inner subtyping can also be used to subtype one or more of the alternatives, so that if that alternative is selected, then only a subset of the original values is possible:

```
Class3PDU ::= TransportProtocolPDU
    (
        WITH COMPONENTS
        {...,
            data                (INCLUDES NormalDT),
            dataAck             (INCLUDES NormalAK),
            expeditedData       (INCLUDES NormalED),
            expeditedDataAck    (INCLUDES NormalEA),
            reject              (INCLUDES NormalRJ),
        }
    )
```

4.2.5   Any

The values of the **any type** are all of the values of all possible ASN.1 types, whether built-in or defined. Thus, it can be used to describe a "hole" in the specification of an abstract syntax, needed where it cannot be determined at specification time what actual ASN.1 type is to govern the value which appears there.

The basic type notation is simply the keyword **ANY**. The value notation consists of the notation for the actual value, preceded by the specific ASN.1 type which governs it.[21]

Thus, for example:

```
v1 ANY ::= INTEGER 505
v2 ANY ::= SET{a BOOLEAN, b NULL} {a TRUE, b NULL}
```

Because the any type includes all possible ASN.1 types, it is not distinct from any other type, and so cannot be used in a context where distinctness is needed. Thus, it is not possible to have **ANY** as a component of a set or choice type, or where distinct types are required within a sequence type with optional components. In the case of set or choice, it is possible to have **ANY** as the only component:

```
Useless ::= SET{ANY}
```

but such a data type would seem to serve no practical purpose.

---

[21]   the inclusion of a colon (":") separator between the type and the value is being considered as a possible future extension, as described in 9.1.

In the case of a sequence type, there is no problem, provided the any type does not immediately follow an optional component, and, if optional itself, is the last (or only) component. The following is, therefore, legal:

```
Legal ::= SEQUENCE
    {
        a    INTEGER OPTIONAL,
        b    BOOLEAN,
        c    ANY OPTIONAL
    }
```

Of course, as with the choice type, there is no problem with distinctness, and indeed no need to worry about checking, if the component is itself tagged.

Normally, there is additional information carried along with the any value which allows the actual type concerned to be identified. The **DEFINED BY** construct allows a linkage to be established between two components of a set or sequence type: the component which is **ANY** and the component which can be used to identify the actual type governing the value to be found there. The linkage is established by including, immediately following the **ANY**, the keywords **DEFINED BY**, and then the identifier of the identifying component.

For example:

```
AttributeValueAssertion ::= SEQUENCE
    {
        attributeType INTEGER,
        attributeValue ANY DEFINED BY attributeType
    }
```

This implies that the value of the **attributeType** component must unambiguously determine the actual type governing the value in the **attributeValue**. For example, it could be that if the **attributeType** component takes the value **63**, then the **attributeValue** component must take a **PrintableString (SIZE (8))** value.

A value conforming to this constraint is as follows:

```
v AttributeValueAssertion ::=
{
    attributeType      63,
    attributeValue     PrintableString (SIZE(8)) "Quincunx"
}
```

The component which is identified by the **ANY DEFINED BY** construct (**attributeType** in the example) can be viewed as an index into some list or register, which for each index value, specifies the actual type of the any value.

This index can be either an integer or an object identifier; in the former case when a single list under the control of a single authority is envisaged, in the latter when an open-ended collection of authorities is involved.

There is presently no notational support in ASN.1 for specifying which types correspond to which index values, and many existing applications make use of ASN.1 macros (see Chapter 5) for this purpose. However, there are likely to be some enhancements in this area, from the work described in 9.2 below.

The use of **ANY** without the **DEFINED BY** construct is "deprecated" (frowned upon) by the standard. However there are presently a number of limitations with the latter construct which mean that some "naked" **ANY**s may be inevitable.

These limitations include the fact that **ANY DEFINED BY** can only appear as a (possibly tagged) component of a set or sequence type. Thus, for example, it is not possible to have **SEQUENCE OF ANY DEFINED BY** if there is supposed to be a list of values of the indicated type. It is also not possible to use **DEFINED BY** along with a defined type which happens to be the any type.

The identifier must designate another component of the same set or sequence type. Thus, where there are nested sequences and sets, reference outwards or inwards is not possible.

The component so designated, and which indicates the type must be *"either an integer type or an object identifier type"* (ISO 8824 revised) or *"an integer type or an enumerated type or an object identifier type or a type derived from those by tagging or subtyping"* (X.208).[22] While X.208 is rather more liberal, allowing both tagging and subtyping (rightly) and enumerated (probably wrongly), neither allows the reasonable possibility of a choice type whose alternatives are integer and object identifier.

To subtype the any type, the single value and contained subtype constructs are available. There are some problems with this however.[23] Firstly, this allows some bizarre types to be defined, such as:

```
Dangerous ::= ANY
(
    [0] IMPLICIT INTEGER 0
|   [0] IMPLICIT BOOLEAN FALSE
)
```

in which the two values have identical BER encodings, and thus are indistinguishable. Secondly, the definition of contained subtype

---

[22]   this discrepancy between the ISO/IEC and CCITT versions, one of a very few that managed to creep in, will be resolved by correcting one or both of the specifications.

[23]   Both presently the subject of defect reports (see 9.1).

seems to preclude perhaps the most obvious form of subtyping for any, namely restricting it to the values of some *bona fide* ASN.1 type.

Thus, we might want to say:

```
General ::= SEQUENCE
{
    a    INTEGER,
    b    ANY
}
Specific ::= General
(WITH COMPONENTS{
    a    (0..MAX),
    b    (INCLUDES IA5String)
})
```

However, a contained subtype is supposed to have been defined as a subtype of the same parent type, in this case any, which is not true of IA5String. With this retriction, it is actually impossible to define a subtype of any which is not built up directly or indirectly, from single values.

In retrospect, it might have been better for any not to have been described as a type. Considered as a type, it certainly has some strange properties. The work on macro replacement (see 9.2 below) may well remove the concept of an any *type*, while preserving the underlying ability to have components of open-ended type.

4.2.6 Tagged

So far we have seen the use of tagging to ensure distinctness among the components of sets, choices and sequences with optional components.

However, precisely what does it mean for two components to be distinct from each other? Which of the following pairs are distinct?

INTEGER	BOOLEAN
INTEGER (0..5)	INTEGER (6..10)

ENUMERATED
{
    low (0),
    medium (1),
    high (2)
}
	ENUMERATED
	{
	    yes (1),
	    no (-1),
	    dontKnow (0)
	}

SEQUENCE
    {INTEGER, BOOLEAN}
	SEQUENCE
	    {BOOLEAN, INTEGER}

SET
    {INTEGER, BOOLEAN}
	SET OF CHOICE
	    {INTEGER, BOOLEAN}

INTEGER	ANY

The answer, which may seem surprising, is that only the first pair are distinct in this sense. Fortunately, the rule is a simple one: two component types are distinct if and only if their **tags** are distinct.

In this regard, every ASN.1 type, whether built-in or defined, has a tag, except for choice types which have a tag for each of their alternatives, and the any type which has all possible tags. Two types are distinct if they have no tags in common. (It can thus be easily seen why any is not distinct from any other type).

There are four distinct classes of tag, and each tag within its class is numbered with a non-negative integer. The four classes are: universal, context-specific, application-wide, and private-use.

All of the built-in types have tags in the **universal** class. These tags generally do not appear in the notation, and it is rarely necessary for users of the notation to have any awareness of them. Thus, for example, the integer type has the tag number 2 in the universal class, as do all its subtypes.

The assignment of all of the tags in the universal class can be seen in Appendix F. It is necessary to remember only that, in general, universal tags are in one-to-one correspondence to the keyword(s) which start the type notation. The only exceptions to this are:

- sequence types and sequence-of types all have the same tag[24];
- set types and set-of types all have the same tag;
- choice types have all the tags of their alternatives;
- the any type has all tags of all classes.

The tags of all classes other than universal are available to abstract syntax designers to form **tagged types**. A tagged type is based upon another (base) type and has the same information-bearing capacity but has a new tag. Thus, a tagged integer type has the same number of values as does the integer type, and can be used for all the same purposes, but has some tag other than number 2 in the universal class.[25]

---

[24] This is for historical reasons: in X.409, sequence and sequence-of were considered just different varieties of the same type. (This also applies to set and set-of).

[25] Another way of expressing this is that a type and all of the possible tagged types based upon it are **isomorphic**, there being a 1-1 correspondence between their values.

We have already seen the use of tagged types of the **context-specific** class; they are formed from a number (the tag number) in square brackets ("[]"), and followed by the base type. Thus, in:

```
TypC ::= SET
{
      t      [0]   INTEGER,
      u      [1]   INTEGER,
      v      [2]   BOOLEAN
}
```

there are three tagged types with context-specific tags.

The context-specific tags are used in just the way we have seen, for achieving local distinctness of components of sets and sequences and choices. The same tag can be reused as many times as required, subject only to the distinctness rules. Thus:

```
CanDo ::= SET {
             a    [0]   CHOICE{
                          b    [0]   INTEGER,
                          c    [1]   BOOLEAN},
             d    [1]   SET{
                          e    [0]   REAL,
                          f    [1]   BOOLEAN}}
```

which uses the context-specific tags number 0 and 1 three times each, is perfectly correct, because they are each used only once for the components of a particular set or choice type.

Although it is not precluded, it is usually unwise to assign type references to tagged types of this class. Thus, in preference to:

```
TransportProtocolPDU ::= CHOICE
      {
            connectionRequest    CR,
            connectionConfirm    CC,
            ...
      }
CR ::= [0] SET {...}
CC ::= [1] SET {...}
```

in which the individual PDU definitions incorporate the tags, use:

```
TransportProtocolPDU ::= CHOICE
      {
            connectionRequest    [0]  CR,
            connectionConfirm    [1]  CC,
            ...
      }
CR ::= SET {...}
CC ::= SET {...}
```

in which the tags are explicitly displayed within the choice type. This eases the correct management of the distinctness of the tags.

The other two classes of tags are of marginal utility, and should generally be avoided. The **application-wide** tags were intended to be used for types expected to be of common utility across a whole application protocol or protocol family. The idea was that such types would be defined as tagged types of the application-wide class, and thereafter could be used in sets, sequences and choices, safe in the knowledge that they were distinct from all universal types. Defining such a tagged type involves the same notation as for context-specific, except that the keyword **APPLICATION** appears between the "[" and the number.

Thus, within some application, there might be a collection of definitions:

```
Temperature ::=    [APPLICATION 0] INTEGER (-100..60)
Pressure ::=       [APPLICATION 1] INTEGER (850..1100)
Humidity ::=       [APPLICATION 2] INTEGER (0..100)
```

with no two such definitions having the same application-wide tag.

They could then be used within sets and choices without having to be retagged each time, thus:

```
AtmosphericReading ::= SET
    {
        height            INTEGER (0..60000)
                             -- metres above sea-level --,
        temperature       Temperature,
        pressure          Pressure,
        humidity          Humidity
    }
```

All of these components, despite functionally being integers, are distinct. However, notwithstanding this, there will still be cases where more than one component of a set is inherently of the same type, and where recourse to context-specific tags will be necessary:

```
TemperatureRange ::= SET
    {
        minimum      [0]  Temperature,
        average      [1]  Temperature,
        maximum      [2]  Temperature
    }
```

It was also envisaged that this would allow implementations to analyse incoming messages more readily, for example to check that every value which purported to be a **Temperature**, no matter where it might be found, would always be an integer in the appropriate range. However, there are problems with this also.

One arises from the ability to import and export definitions at will, which makes it very difficult to ensure that application-wide tags are really unique throughout an entire protocol. Another is that recognition depends on the tag actually being carried in the encoding, which is not always so. In particular, it is not so when the tag is *implicit*, as described below.

There is also some confusion about the scope of uniqueness of application-wide tags. In one place in the ASN.1 specification, it is said to be the module, in another, the *"standard or Recommendation"* (i.e. a specification). In resolving this, it is likely in the future that ASN.1 will remove the restrictions on the uniqueness of application-wide tags, leaving only the rule that tags must be distinct within a set or choice. It will only be *suggested* that they be managed so as to be unique across some application, as defined by the user of the notation.

The fourth and last class of tags are the **private-use** tags. These tags were intended to be used by an organisation to produce an extended version of some protocol under the control of another (like a standards body) and which is not to clash with any subsequent extension which might be made by the other organisation. The notation is similar to that for application-wide tags, except that the keyword **PRIVATE** is employed.

Thus, assuming that we have a type **RejectTPDU** defined in some standard, as in 4.2.1 above, namely:

```
RejectTPDU ::= SET
{
    destRef      [0]  Reference,
    yr-tu-nr     [1]  TPDUnumber,
    credit       [2]  Credit
}
```

someone could define a proprietary version:

```
MyRejectTPDU ::= SET
{
    destRef      [0]  Reference,
    yr-tu-nr     [1]  TPDUnumber,
    credit       [2]  Credit,
    extended     [PRIVATE 0] BOOLEAN DEFAULT FALSE
}
```

The extended protocol is not, in general, conformant to the original protocol but is just derived from it.

The assumption behind the use of a private-use tag here is that it would have been inappropriate to have carried out the extension by use of a tagged type of any other class (for example **[3]**), because a subsequent version of the standard might have used that same tag for some other purpose. However, this would only be a problem if the intent was automatically to extend the new version of the standard in the same way, and in general, this is not possible, as the standard and proprietary extensions may interfere in some way.

Much better in general is to extend the standard in ways that the standard has envisaged, in which case there will be components, often involving **ANY**, which are there for precisely the purpose of extension. In such places there is of course no need to have recourse to private-use tags.

Again, as stated above, application-wide and private tags should be avoided if possible.

The **minimum** component of **TemperatureRange** above has the type:

```
[0] Temperature
```

but **Temperature** is a defined type, so **minimum** is further equivalent to:

```
[0] [APPLICATION 0] INTEGER (-100..60)
```

How many tags does this component have? It would seem, on the face of it, to have three: context-specific number 0, application-wide number 0, and universal number 2. However, from the distinctness point-of-view it has only one, namely the outermost (leftmost) one, which is context-specific number 0.

It is permitted in ASN.1 to write down something like:

```
Useless ::= [0] [APPLICATION 17] [1] [0] [0] INTEGER
```

however, this is not really of any use, and if there are nested tags, it is much more likely to arise as described for the **minimum** component of **TemperatureRange**.

Although only the outermost tag is significant for distinctness purposes, the inner tags may also be represented in the encoded value. This depends on whether the tags are applied implicitly or explicitly (and on the encoding rules in use).

Every tag is either **implicit** or **explicit**. The selection can be made in the tagged type notation by including the keyword **IMPLICIT** or **EXPLICIT** following the "]" and preceding the base type. If neither keyword appears (as for all the examples so far) then the tag style default, as selected at the head of the module, applies.

The tag style default appears just after the keyword **DEFINITION** at the head of the module. It may be **IMPLICIT TAGS**, in which case implicit tagging is the default, or may be **EXPLICIT TAGS** or omitted, in which case explicit tagging is the default.[26]

---

26   In X.409, and in the first version of the ASN.1 standard, there was no way of changing the tag style default, which was that tags should be explicit, and only the **IMPLICIT** keyword was provided.

Thus, if the tag style default were **EXPLICIT TAGS** then the components of a set could be tagged implicitly as follows:

```
RejectTPDU ::= SET
{
    destRef        [0] IMPLICIT Reference,
    yr-tu-nr       [1] IMPLICIT TPDUnumber,
    credit         [2] IMPLICIT Credit
}
```

It should be noted carefully that the keyword **IMPLICIT** qualifies the tag, not the base type. It only appears following the "]". A mistake that many ASN.1 beginners make (and this has even appeared in some draft standards!) is to write something like:

Illegal ::= IMPLICIT INTEGER

So what is the distinction between implicit and explicit tagging?

Well, unfortunately, the primary distinction is in the encoding, and thus it is not really appropriate for it to be in ASN.1 at all. When a tag is applied implicitly, the encoding rules may be defined to replace the inner tag with the new one. (The ASN.1 Basic Encoding Rules take advantage of this). When the tag is applied explicitly, the encoding rules are supposed to carry both the old and the new tags. (The BER do so).

The effect is that implicit tagging is slightly more economical than explicit tagging in the BER encoding, and the price paid is the sacrifice of some opportunities for extension, and strong type checking. The opportunities for extension arise from the fact that encoding rules for ASN.1 are supposed to produce the same encoding for the following two values:

```
v1 [0] EXPLICIT INTEGER ::= 5
```

and

```
v2 [0] CHOICE {integer INTEGER, real REAL} ::= integer 5
```

(what was a single type, **INTEGER**, has been extended to a choice type, of which **INTEGER** is one of the alternatives). Thus a backwards-compatible extension of the protocol has been made, and in the most natural way, by simply replacing the **INTEGER** by the choice type *in situ*.

However, the value:

```
v3 [0] IMPLICIT INTEGER ::= 5
```

would be encoded differently. In fact it would be illegal in the notation to replace **INTEGER** with **CHOICE{...}** if the former were implicitly tagged. That is because with a choice type, the distinction between the alternatives is achieved by means of their tags. The implication of implicit tagging, that the old tag could be replaced by the (single) new one is clearly meaningless, and therefore disallowed, for choice types (and thus also for the any type). Where implicit tagging is the default, it is automatically disabled for choice types and any.

It was suggested in 4.2.5 above that if extensions of this kind are envisaged, then choice types with only one alternative should be used. This exploits the fact that, even if implicit tagging is the default, the value:

```
v0 [0] CHOICE {integer INTEGER} ::= integer 5
```

has the same encoding as **v1** and **v2**. However, the trouble with that approach is that it is not always possible to predict all of the places where extension of this kind would prove to be necessary.

In practice, the keyword **IMPLICIT** and **EXPLICIT** need very rarely be used, because designers tend to be "implicit taggers" or "explicit taggers" by inclination, they set the default accordingly, and then allow the chosen default to take effect everywhere.

This author is inclined to be an "explicit tagger" because of the horrendous effects on the evolvability of a particular protocol caused by an ill-considered implicit tag in the initial version.

In retrospect, this whole issue should have been omitted altogether from the notation, with different encoding rules being chosen according to whether or not the compactness offered by implicit tagging was important.

4.3 Useful types

There are several types which are defined in the ASN.1 specification using ASN.1 itself, and which are made available to users by means of type references assigned to them. These types are referred to as the **useful types** because although they could (almost) have been defined by a user of the notation, they were deemed to be generally useful.

Although ASN.1 is rather unclear on the subject, the type references of the useful types should be regarded as reserved, and not reused - rather as if the definitions were included in every module.

The single respect in which the ordinary designer could not have designed the useful types is that they have universal tags, and there is no way for a designer to assign those. Within the ASN.1 specification itself, there is one extension to the notation to allow for this, a piece of notation which is permitted nowhere else. That extension is the ability to use the keyword **UNIVERSAL** in defining a tagged type, in the same place as the ordinary designer can use **APPLICATION** or **PRIVATE**.

The following is an example of such a definition taken from the
ASN.1 specification:

```
ObjectDescriptor ::=
                [UNIVERSAL 7] IMPLICIT GraphicString
```

To repeat, this can only be done within the ASN.1 specification itself,
and is not available to the general user of the notation.

There are presently four useful types. Two of them are concerned
with representing date and time (Generalized time, Universal time);
one with embedding values from other abstract syntaxes in an ASN.1
type (External); and one with providing a human-readable
counterpart to the object identifier type (Object descriptor).

The value notation and subtype possibilities for the useful types
can be inferred from their ASN.1 definitions. The definitions of the
useful types are shown in Appendix G.

4.3.1   Generalized time

The **generalized time type** can be used to carry a time and date
in textual form. The type has the pre-defined type reference
GeneralizedTime (note the spelling of "Generalized"). The
representation is based upon a series of ISO standards (presently
being encompassed by a single one). In essence, the representation
used is YYYYMMDDHHMMSS.SSS although the precision can vary,
and an indication of the time differential between local and universal
time can be appended.

The same moment, 5 minutes and 33.8 seconds after 7 a.m. on
2nd January, 1982 in New York City, can be represented as:

```
moment-L      GeneralizedTime ::=      "19820102070533.8"
moment-U      GeneralizedTime ::=      "19820102120533.8Z"
moment-LU     GeneralizedTime ::=      "19820102070533.8-0500"
```

4.3.2   Universal time

The **universal time type**, actually known by the built-in type
reference **UTCTime**, is intended for use in international applications
where the local time alone is not adequate, and the flexibility to use
all of the forms allowed by **GeneralizedTime** is not required.

The constraints are that the year is specified by two digits (the
low-order digits of the Christian-era year), the time is specified to a
precision of either 1 minute or 1 second, and either Z or a time
differential (+HHMM or -HHMM) must be appended.

For example:

```
moment       UTCTime ::=             "8201020706-0500"
```

4.3.3   External

The **external type**, actually named **EXTERNAL**, can be used to embed, within a value of one abstract syntax, a value from another abstract syntax. The value to be embedded may or may not be a value of an ASN.1 type. For example:

```
FileContents ::= EXTERNAL
```

The definition of the type can be seen in Appendix G. In essence, each of its values comprises an encoding together with reference information which allows that encoding to be interpreted.

The reference information can be either a direct reference, an indirect reference, or both. The indirect reference, if present, identifies a presentation context (see 7.2) governing the interpretation of the encoding. The direct reference is an object identifier value. If the reference information only includes a direct reference, then this is taken to identify an abstract syntax and an associated transfer syntax. If both references are present, the direct reference is taken to identify the transfer syntax only. This only arises while presentation context establishment is incomplete.

There are three possibilities for the encoding: single ASN.1 type, octet-aligned and arbitrary. If the value being embedded is a single ASN.1 value, and is encoded using the same encoding rules as the overall external value, then any of the three possibilities can be used. If the value is not an ASN.1 value, or is encoded using different encoding rules, but is known to be an integral number of octets in length, then either of the latter two possibilities can be used. If the encoding is not an integral number of octets, then only the third possibility can be used.

The external type is more flexible and safer, but also much less efficient, than the any, octet string or bit string types which can also be used directly to embed values defined elsewhere. It is indispensable if embedded presentation data values are to be conveyed.

As it turns out, there are actually two subtly different capabilities lumped together as the external type. The work in progress on macro replacement has identified this fact, and consideration is being given to superseding the present **EXTERNAL** notation with something which better reflects the dichotomy, while retaining backwards compatibility.

The two cases are, firstly, the embedding of values from different presentation contexts, and, secondly, the embedding of values from particular information objects. In the first case the indirect reference is always present, while in the second it is always absent.

If permitted by the designer (it almost never is) an object descriptor (see 4.3.4) may also appear in the external value.

4.3.4   Object descriptor

The **object descriptor type** was added to ASN.1 at the same time as the object identifier type. The idea was that, while the latter is a machine-oriented identification of an information object, there might be a need for a human-oriented textual description. Thus it is recommended that when an object identifier value is allocated to some information object, an object descriptor should also be allocated.

If an application needs to carry one of these textual descriptions, it describes the appropriate field as **ObjectDescriptor**. For example:

```
whizzoSpread ObjectDescriptor ::=
    "Whizzo Corp's Spiffy Spreadsheet File Format V3.09"
```

As it turns out, most information objects are such that it is not really sensible to allocate, or to carry around, human-readable descriptions, so the above recommendation has generally gone unheeded.

5 Macros

This chapter describes the macro capability and its application.

5.1 Introduction

ASN.1 provides a mechanism whereby users can extend the notation for their own use, or for use by others. A user extending the notation does so by defining one or more **macros**, using the **macro definition notation** (MDN). Each macro has a macro reference (like a type reference except that all letters, not just the first, must be in upper-case), and grammars for type and value notation. These grammars are defined by the macro designer using BNF.

A macro definition can be imported and exported by means of its macroreference, just as with type and value definitions.

To the macro user, the macro appears to introduce a new kind of ASN.1 type with its own notation. The new type notation can be used wherever in ASN.1 a type can appear, and the new value notation can be used wherever a value (of that type) can appear. Macros do not, however, introduce any new types or values as far as encoding rules go. For that purpose, each value of a macro type turns out to be equivalent to a value from some ordinary ASN.1 type, the **delivered value**.

It is this equivalence which led to the use of the term "macro" for the capability. However it is important to realise that it does not involve the kind of text substitution provided by, say, the macro capability in the "C" preprocessor, or by macro-processors such as ML/1.

Instead, the macro designer "programs" the macro to deliver a value of some ASN.1 type. The value delivered (and possibly its type) will often depend on the actual type and value notation (conforming to the grammars) which was supplied by the macro user.

Consider the following relatively straightforward example of a macro definition[27]:

---

[27] This macro follows CCITT Recommendation X.208, in which value references within macros start with a lower-case letter, the same as outside macros. ISO 8824 demands that value references within macros start with upper-case letters.

71

```
POSSIBLE MACRO ::= BEGIN

TYPE NOTATION ::=
    type (X)
        <PossibleX ::= CHOICE {present X, omitted NULL}>

VALUE NOTATION ::=
    "OMITTED"
        <VALUE PossibleX ::= omitted NULL> |
    value (x X)
        <VALUE PossibleX ::= present x>

END
```

This macro allows the user to write **POSSIBLE   INTEGER** (or **POSSIBLE   REAL** or whatever) for a type whose allowed values are **OMITTED** together with the **INTEGER** (or **REAL** or whatever) values.

Thus the user could write:

```
A ::= POSSIBLE SEQUENCE OF INTEGER
a1 A ::= OMITTED
a2 A ::= {1, 2, 0}
```

(Of course this macro is completely unnecessary in practice: it would be much better to use directly the choice type which this macro delivers. That is also likely to be true of all macros this simple).

The way it works is that after the "::=" in the definition of **A** is an instance of the type notation of **POSSIBLE**. (The type notation always starts with the macro reference itself, which is actually what indicates that macro notation is involved).

As can be seen from the grammar for the type notation of **POSSIBLE**, what is expected next is a type. That is fine, because there *is* a type, namely "**SEQUENCE   OF   INTEGER**". The macro definition further assigns that type the type reference **X** within the macro. (That is what the **X** in parentheses after "**type**" means). So, this macro now includes a hidden definition **X ::= SEQUENCE   OF   INTEGER**. Inside the "<>" we now have another definition, which defines **PossibleX** as a choice of **X** or **NULL**. The former case models the presence of a value of the chosen type, the latter its omission.

We now know that **A** is a type defined by means of the **POSSIBLE** macro, and that there are the following hidden definitions associated with it:

```
X ::= SEQUENCE OF INTEGER
PossibleX ::= CHOICE {present X, omitted NULL}
```

Now we come to the value notation for **A**, which appears after the "::=" in the definitions of **a1** and **a2**. We have to know that it's value notation for a macro type by context; there is no distinguishing prefix, as with the type notation. Looking at the grammar for the value notation, we see that there are two possibilities, separated by "|". The first of these is simply the string "OMITTED". It is this alternative which is taken in the definition of **a1**. When that alternative is taken, the definition:

```
VALUE PossibleX ::= omitted NULL
```

comes into effect. This looks strange, because surely this is a value definition and yet the value reference starts with an upper-case letter. In fact "**VALUE**" is a keyword which appears as a special value reference. It identifies the value to be delivered, which in this case is the value **omitted NULL**, of type **PossibleX**. Normally the assignment to **VALUE** is the last thing the macro definition does.

Note here that the type reference **PossibleX** has been used in defining the value notation. It refers to the definition that was made during the processing of the type notation. Choices taken in the type notation can thus influence the value notation.

The definition of **a2** takes the other alternative for the value notation. Here the value notation is simply defined to be a value of type **X**, which is assigned the value reference **x** within the macro. (That is what the **x X** in parentheses after "**value**" means). That is fine, because there *is* such a value, namely {1, 2, 0}. So, this macro now includes a hidden definition **x X ::=** {1, 2, 0}.

Inside the "<>" we now have another definition:

```
VALUE PossibleX ::= present x
```

which assigns the value **x**, namely {1, 2, 0} to the special value reference **VALUE**, and thus makes it the delivered value.

The various degrees of freedom available to macro designers are described in more detail below. The most important responsibility which macro designers must have is to design macros only when it is really necessary to do so. An example of an unnecessary macro is **POSSIBLE**.

All that would have been necessary was to define a choice type directly:

```
A ::= CHOICE {SEQUENCE OF INTEGER, NULL}
a1 A ::= NULL
a2 A ::= {1, 2, 0}
```

While this may not have the exact notation that the designer would have preferred, it has the advantage that readers familiar with ASN.1 can understand it straight away. With the use of macros, readers have first to understand the macro definitions (requiring them to know BNF) before they can understand the ASN.1.

That said, there are a small number of situations where macros are very useful, and they have been exploited as such in some of the OSI standards. The situations concerned, and the subset of macros which are employed, are described in 5.3 below.

5.2   Macro definition notation

The example macro **POSSIBLE** above showed many but not all of the features of the MDN. The basic idea was shown, namely that the designer defines a macro by supplying grammars for the type and value notation.

When necessary, these grammars are used to recognise strings of characters, within an ASN.1 module, which purport to be type or value notation. As the recognition proceeds, various ASN.1 definitions take effect. These can depend on previous definitions. The recognition of the value notation begins with the definitions made in the type notation in effect. At the end, the delivered value is the one which was assigned to the special value reference **VALUE**.

The overall notation for defining a macro consists of the macro reference, the keyword **MACRO**, the ubiquitous ":=" and then the definition of the grammars. The latter can simply be done by naming another macro, in which case the new macro is identical to the other, except for the macro reference. Ultimately, such a chain of references must lead to a macro whose type and value notation have been defined explicitly.

The definition of the grammars is done in BNF, with various special terminal symbols available to the designer. There is one **production** for the type notation, and one for the value notation, they are the first and second productions respectively). There are as many others as are necessary to define the complete syntax. The complete set of productions is enclosed between **BEGIN** and **END**.

Each production starts with its name. Except for the first two, whose names are "**TYPE NOTATION**" and "**VALUE NOTATION**" respectively, the name is a production reference, which is syntactically the same as a type reference, The name is followed by ":=" followed by one or more alternatives separated by "|". Each alternative is a list of items and/or embedded definitions and/or the names of subsidiary productions.

. To recognise an alternative, the various items and subsidiary productions must be recognised in order in the purported type or value notation.

Each item available to the designer has a corresponding string of characters which it recognises, as follows:

"aaaa"	the string of characters "aaaa" (excluding the double quotes)
string	any sequence of characters (delimited by the item following)
identifier	a string obeying the rules for identifiers or references
number	a string of digits
empty	null string (always recognised)
type	any string which can be recognised as ASN.1 type notation
type (typereference)	as above, but as a side effect of reconition, the type is assigned to the typereference
value (type)	any string which can be recognised as ASN.1 value notation for the type
value (valuereference type)	as above, but as a side effect of recognition, the value is assigned to the valuereference[28]

Items may be separated from each other by spaces and new lines.

Where the name of a subsidiary production appears, then one of the alternatives of that production must be recognised at that point. This may well be recursive, as a production may directly or indirectly include itself as part of an alternative.

Embedded definitions are simply a series of ASN.1 type and value assignments, within "<>". They come into effect at the point in the alternative where they appear. A definition can be superseded by a later assignment to the same reference, and will be deleted if that alternative fails to be completely recognised (i.e. proves to be a blind alley). This, together with the use of items whose recognition causes definitions as a side effect, allows a degree of context sensitivity in the grammar.

5.3 Application of macros

The macro capability provides fairly powerful abilities for the definition of new type and value notation within ASN.1 modules, with the full power of BNF available to the designer, as well as some powerful built-in symbols, such as for types and values. However, much of the macro capability is a syntactic dead-end street; all sorts

---

[28]   Here, and in "embedded definitions", ISO 8824, but not X.208, states that value references should start with *upper-case* letters. The reason for this is lost in the mists of time. The inconsistency will be resolved; however, both possibilities may be encountered in existing specifications.

of symbols can be recognised but not much can be done with them afterwards. After all, the total upshot of using the new notation, as far as ASN.1 is concerned, is the delivered value, and its type.

Consider the following macro, for example, which appears in the standard for Remote Operations (ROS)[29]:

```
OPERATION MACRO ::=
BEGIN
TYPE NOTATION          ::= Argument   Result   Errors
VALUE NOTATION         ::= value (VALUE OperationCode)

Argument               ::= "ARGUMENT" type  | empty
Result                 ::= "RESULT" ResultType  |  empty
Errors                 ::= "ERRORS" "{" ErrorName "}"  |  empty

ResultType             ::= type | empty
ErrorNames             ::= ErrorList | empty
ErrorList              ::= Error  | ErrorList  ","  Error
Error                  ::= value (ERROR)
END

OperationCode ::= INTEGER
```

A typical example of the use of this macro is as follows:

```
get OPERATION
        ARGUMENT    AttributeType
        RESULT      ArgumentValue
        ERRORS      {noSuchAttribute, accessBarred}
   ::=  5
```

This is a value assignment of the following pattern:

```
get  OPERATION ... accessBarred}   ::=  5
```

where the material "**OPERATION** ... **accessBarred}**" is valid type notation introduced by the **OPERATION** macro, and "5" is the value notation.

This looks as though a lot is going on. Several types and values are recognised; various keywords may or may not be present; there is a list of error names which can be empty or can have an arbitrary number of members. However, the "bottom-line" of the whole thing, as far as ASN.1 is concerned, is the delivered value, namely the **INTEGER** value 5. Furthermore, that value is directly supplied by the user, and does not even arise from any cunning program devised by macro designer.

As far as ASN.1 goes, it would seem that the above is no different from:

```
get INTEGER ::= 5
```

---

[29]   A number of details have been omitted here for the sake of simplicity.

The difference is clear, however, when we examine what the purpose of the **OPERATION** macro is, namely to allow users of ROS to define operations using a well-defined notation. The **OPERATION** macro is supplied by the designers of ROS, and defines that notation. It clearly defines the degrees of freedom available to ROS users: they can define an argument data type introduced by the keyword "**ARGUMENT**"; they can define a result data type introduced by the keyword "**RESULT**"; and so on.

The value notation for **OPERATION** is simply an integer value, and allows the ROS user to allocate an **OperationCode** value to the operation. That value happens to be the delivered value, so that if the macro appears in a PDU definition, it is the integer value which is actually sent.

The result is that the macro defines a kind of definition form or template for a concept, in this case "operation", which is more complex than just an ASN.1 type and value. In fact it is an assemblage of related types and values, related through being aspects of the same operation.

Such a form or template could clearly have been defined by means outside of ASN.1. However, because many or all of the aspects of such a concept *are* specified using ASN.1, it proves very convenient to be able to include the definition within an ASN.1 module along with the definitions of the types and values involved. Furthermore, because the use of macros results in ASN.1 types and values, they can be given reference names, can be included in modules, and can be imported and exported using all of the same mechanisms already provided in ASN.1.

One could perhaps argue that this can be done without using macros. For example, the following might replace the above definitions:

```
get OperationCode ::= 5
GetArgument ::= AttributeType
GetResult ::= AttributeValue
GetErrors ::= ErrorCode (noSuchAttribute | accessBarred)
```

where:

```
noSuchAttribute ErrorCode      ::= 1 -- let's say
accessBarred ErrorCode         ::= 2 -- let's say
```

However, only the similar names of the types and values relates them together as being for the same operation, whereas the macro groups all of these aspects together. There is also no name for the whole assemblage, as there is with macros.

The foregoing is the predominant usage of macros in existing standards. The macro corresponds to some concept, more complex than a data type, of which users can define instances. The type notation defines the form or template, with all of the appropriate degrees of freedom provided. The value notation is almost always an integer or object identifier value which is the delivered value, and which constitutes the "run-time" identification of the instance.

As a matter of fact the whole idea of the macro notation originated with the operation concept back in 1983. CCITT planned to add notation to ASN.1 (X.409 as it was then) to define an **OPERATION** data type. ISO were in the process of adopting the technical content of X.409, but were reluctant to include such a type. The agreement was that a macro capability would be added which would allow CCITT to define the **OPERATION** notation, without it being added directly to ASN.1.

Subsequently, the macro capability has become perhaps the most maligned part of ASN.1. The maligning has not always been justified. However, there are a number of difficulties with the macro capability as it is.

For one thing, the text describing it, Annex A of the standard, is widely regarded as impenetrable. As an example, it includes the following single-sentence paragraph:

> "The resulting type and value of an instance of use of the new value notation is determined by the value (and the type of the value) finally assigned to the distinguished local value reference identified by the keyword VALUE, according to the processing of the macrodefinition for the new type notation followed by that for the new value notation".

(Of course having read this far, you can now can understand that: right ?)

There are also a number of known, if minor, bugs in the text, and a number of ambiguities.

The most serious problem, however, is probably the fact that the macro capability seems to promise more than it delivers. One might expect, for example, that the **OPERATION** macro designer would be able to do something with the argument data type provided by the user, for instance use it in defining some PDU. However, this is not possible: that data type is constrained to be present in the notation but nothing happens to it, and there is not even any way of referring to it outside of the macro itself.

There are now plans to provide a more satisfactory way of defining information objects which are assemblages of types and values. This is discussed a little further in Chapter 9. It may eventually lead to the dropping of the macro capability from ASN.1.

6 The Basic Encoding Rules

This chapter describes the ASN.1 Basic Encoding Rules (BER).

6.1 Overview

The original CCITT Recommendation X.409, which first standardised the notation now known as ASN.1, included both the notation and a set of encoding rules. The intent of the designers of X.409 back in 1983 was to define a universal set of encoding rules which could be built into every system, and used everywhere. Encoding would simply cease to become an issue in protocol design. Interestingly, there was another attempt in the early 1980s to promote a universal way of encoding protocol data, and this was proposed at one stage to be used for all of the OSI layers.[30] It failed for a number of non-technical reasons. However it likely would not have been a rival for the X.409 encoding as, for one thing, there was no associated notation.

Meanwhile, over in the OSI Committee in ISO, they were busy devoting a whole layer (Presentation) to the job of negotiating transfer syntaxes. If there truly were a universal set of encoding rules, then every such negotiation would be degenerate, and the Presentation Layer worse than useless!

Anyway, when the encoding rules were teased apart from the notation, they were dubbed the Basic Encoding Rules (BER), with the idea that there might be justification for defining different sets of encoding rules. Such encoding rules would not just be different for the sake of being different, but would be designed to meet some functional requirement, such as optimising compactness of encoding at the expense of computational overhead, or vice versa.

It now seems likely (see Chapter 9) that there will indeed be additional standardised encoding rules in the future. (Of course any organisation has always been at liberty to design its own proprietary ones for any reason). Thus, even if every abstract syntax were designed using ASN.1, there would still be a role for the Presentation Layer to negotiate the encoding rules to be used.

---

30   Unfortunately, the author can now find no trace of this scheme, which was proposed by AT&T.

It is worth noting that a clear advantage of the use of encoding rules such as the BER rather than hand-crafting transfer syntaxes is that application designers do not need to be familiar with their details; indeed neither do most implementors. This is analogous with the way that programmers using high-level languages do not have to know in detail how data structures are held in memory. However in both cases it helps to have a general awareness, if for no other reason than to know how "expensive" various constructs are.

The BER generate encodings which are of a class known as type - length - value (TLV), so called because the basis of encoding is a structure made up of those three parts. Many protocols employ encoding schemes of this general kind. However, few apply the idea so consistently as the BER.

With BER, the encoding of every data value in an abstract syntax, whether an entire PDU or some component of it, is constructed in TLV style.[31] The three parts are actually termed identifier (I), length (L) and contents (C).

The **identifier** conveys three pieces of information: the tag class of the data value being conveyed; the tag number; the **form** of the encoding - whether it is **primitive** or **constructed**.

The **length** (together with the form) allows the end of the contents to be found. The receiving system need not understand the tag to find the end of the contents, and this allows an encoding to be skipped if it cannot (yet) be decoded.

The **contents** is the substance of the encoding, conveying the actual value. When the form of the encoding is primitive, the contents is simply a series of octets (zero or more):

When the form is constructed, the contents is a series of nested encodings, each itself having identifier, length and contents, as in:

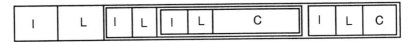

This nesting can be as deep or as shallow as needed; its primary purpose is to convey values which have components which themselves have components, and so on, to any depth.

Nesting stops either with a primitive encoding, or with a constructed encoding with empty contents.

---

31   CCITT Recommendation X.409 referred to such an encoding as a **data element**, however, this term was dropped when joint working with ISO began, because it has different connotations there.

Each part of the encoding (and therefore also the encoding as a whole) is an integral number of octets.

6.2 Identifier

The identifier is the first part of every encoding and occupies an integral number of octets, at least one.

As indicated above, its purpose is to convey the tag (class and number) of the value, and the form of the encoding. ASN.1 does not limit the size of tag numbers: it would be legitimate, though strange and probably ill-advised, to define a type such as:

```
[208326000] INTEGER
```

Accordingly, the identifier does not have a fixed or maximum number of octets allocated to it.

Nonetheless, the vast majority of all tags have relatively small numbers and the design of the identifier octets takes this into account. There are two variants, one employing a single octet and the other multiple octets. Identifiers are always encoded in the minimum number of octets necessary to represent the tag.

The single octet variant of the identifier is used for tag numbers in the range 0-30 inclusive. (This includes all universal tags presently allocated, and will include most if not all context-specific tags if they are solely used for distinguishing types within choices and sets).

The single octet variant is as follows:

```
8 7 6 5 4 3 2 1
C C F T T T T T
       1
```

where the two bit field CC represents the tag class, the single bit F the form, and the five bit field TTTTT the tag number. Where that field takes the value 11111, however, it indicates that the multiple octet variant is being employed.

The multiple octet variant is used when the tag number is greater than 30. It is as follows:

```
8 7 6 5 4 3 2 1  8 7 6 5 4 3 2 1     8 7 6 5 4 3 2 1
C C F 1 1 1 1 1  1 T T T T T T T  •  0 T T T T T T T
       1               2                    n
```

where the $7*(n-1)$ bit field formed by concatenating together, in order, all of the TTTTTTT fields, represents the tag number.

In both variants the various tag classes and form are represented as follows:

bit 8 7	TAG CLASS
0 0	universal
0 1	application-wide
1 0	context-specific
1 1	private-use

bit 6	FORM
0	primitive
1	constructed

The tag number is represented as an unsigned binary number in which lower numbered octets and higher numbered bits are the more significant.

An example of a single octet identifier is:

01100110 (66_{16})

which represents a constructed encoding whose tag class is application-wide and tag number is **6**.

An example of a multiple octet identifier is:

10011111 11100011 10101011 10011010 01110000

($9FE3AB9A70_{16}$)

which represents a primitive encoding whose tag class is context-specific and tag number is **208326000**.

It might be thought that the use of 7-bit fields concatenated together is a rather inefficient way of representing large tags, because it requires a lot of "shifting and or-ing". However there are two reasons why this does not matter.

Firstly, as indicated above, such tags will be rare, and thus any inefficiency is unlikely to be important.

Secondly, and more significantly, the processing mentioned need not actually occur in the running system. That is because, at run-time, the only operation needed on tag numbers is comparison - "does this string of octets comprise the encoding of a value of this data type?". For that purpose the actual integer value of the tag is not needed: the octets of the identifier itself (excluding the form bit) can be used directly.

All that is necessary is that the running system be equipped with knowledge of which identifiers are expected. With the multiple octet example above, the identifier octets:

$9FD3AB9A70_{16}$

can be the basis of comparison, rather than the tag number **208326000**, which happens to be:

$0C6ACD70_{16}$

6.3 Length

The length is the second part of every encoding, coming immediately after the identifier, and occupies an integral number of octets, at least one.

The length field does not always literally represent the length of the contents, but it does always allow the end of the contents to be found (without knowledge of the tag).

The length field has three variants: **short, long** and **indefinite**. (The short and long variants are sometimes referred to as definite). The definite variants encode the length, in octets, of the contents. With the indefinite variant, the end of the contents is indicated by a special marker.

The short variant can be used for any encoding whose contents is 127 octets or less in length, and is as follows:

```
 8 7 6 5 4 3 2 1
| 0 LL LLLLL |
       1
```

where the field LLLLLLL represents, in unsigned binary, the length of the contents.

The long variant can be used for any encoding, and is as follows:

```
 8 7 6 5 4 3 2 1 8 7 6 5 4 3 2 1   8 7 6 5 4 3 2 1
|1| 0 <n  < 127|L L L L L L L L| · |L L L L L L L L|
       1              2                  n +1
```

where the field which in the short form held the length now holds the length of the length, n. The length itself is carried in octets 2 to $n+1$. The value n must be at least one and must be less than 127 (the latter value is reserved for possible extension of the encoding rules).

Notice that there are a number of differences in design between the long variant of the length and the multiple octet variant of the identifier. This is a reflection of different requirements. While the tag numbers represented in the identifier do not need to be recovered at run-time, it *is* necessary for the number of octets to be known. Thus the length is designed to be octet-aligned and not to require any "bit-twiddling" to recover the value. There is also no requirement for the length to be represented in the minimum number of octets. This is because the aim is not comparison, where reducing senders' options is a good thing. Here there are benefits in allowing the sender to choose how many octets to use to represent the length.

Theoretically there is an upper limit on the length of encodings which can be represented by the long form. However the limit is unattainable in practice. The maximum value for n is 126 (wherein the length would be represented in octets 2-127 of the encoding). This provides for 1008 bits to represent the length of the contents, which must therefore be no greater than $2^{1008}-1$ octets, or $2^{1011}-8$ bits long. This truly enormous number is of the order of 10^{313}, compared with the estimated number of electrons in some models of the universe which is 10^{87}.

The indefinite variant can be used for any constructed encoding, and is as follows:

```
 8 7 6 5 4 3 2 1
┌───────────────┐
│1 0 0 0 0 0 0 0│
└───────────────┘
        1
```

This indicates that the **end-of-contents** marker will be found immediately following the last nested encoding. The end-of-contents marker is designed not to be the same as the encoding of any data value. It is as follows:

```
 8 7 6 5 4 3 2 1 8 7 6 5 4 3 2 1
┌───────────────┬───────────────┐
│0 0 0 0 0 0 0 0│0 0 0 0 0 0 0 0│
└───────────────┴───────────────┘
        1               2
```

This has the same representation as would a primitive encoding with universal tag zero and of zero length (no contents octets). However, universal tag zero has deliberately not been allocated to any ASN.1 type.

It should be noted that the indefinite length variant can only be used where the contents is constructed. There, the contents, being a series of nested encodings, is already constrained, and it is possible to define a recognisable end-of-contents marker. Where the contents is primitive, however, any arbitrary bit pattern can appear in the contents octets, and it would not be possible to have an end-of-contents marker. With primitive encodings, therefore, definite length variants must be used.

6.4 Contents

Roughly speaking, the identifier part of an encoding identifies a type, while the contents part identifies one of the (possibly many) values of that type. (In the case of a choice, the identifier also indicates which of the alternatives was selected).

The structure of the contents, therefore, reflects the set of values of the type. For the most part, simple types have primitive encodings, while structured types have constructed encodings. This is perhaps not very surprising, since values of simple types do not have component values, while those of structured types do, by definition.

In 6.5 below we consider each ASN.1 type in turn, and describe the layout of the contents of an encoded value of that type.

The following table summarises the situation, showing, for each of the built-in types of ASN.1, whether the encoding is primitive (P) or constructed (C), and how the various values are represented in the available octets or nested encodings respectively.

INTEGER	P	twos-complement binary number
REAL	P	various possibilities (see below)
NULL	P	no contents octets
BOOLEAN	P	single octet: 00000000=FALSE, any other value=TRUE
ENUMERATED	P	as for integer
BIT STRING	P	the bits of the value (first octet indicates the number of unused bits in the last)
	C	segmented value
OCTET STRING	P	the octets of the value
	C	segmented value
Character strings	P	the octets representing the characters, according to the appropriate standard
	C	segmented value
OBJECT IDENTIFIER	P	packed sequence of numbers representing the arc labels
SET	C	component values, in arbitrary order
SEQUENCE	C	component values, in the definition order
SET OF	C	component values, in arbitrary order
SEQUENCE OF	C	component values, in intended order
CHOICE	P/C	as for type of selected alternative
ANY	P/C	as for type actually used
Tagged (implicit)	P/C	as for base type
(explicit)	C	nested encoding of equivalent untagged value
Useful types	P/C	as defined

6.5 Encodings

This section describes the encoding in detail for each of the built-in types, and provides examples. The universal tags allocated to the various built-in types are listed in Appendix F.

6.5.1 Integer

The encoding of an integer value is primitive, and the contents octets represent the value using a twos-complement binary representation.

In such a representation, where m bits are available to represent a value, the most significant bit has is given a weight of $-(2^{m-1})$. (Lower numbered octets and higher numbered bits are the more significant). All other bits have a positive weight, ranging from 2^{m-2} for the second most significant to 2^0 (=1) for the least significant.

Thus, with two octets (16 bits) to represent a value, the most significant bit is worth -32768 (-2^{15}), the next 16384(2^{14}), then 8192 and so on down to 1. The value:

10010110 01000110

is therefore $-27066=-32768+4096+1024+512+64+4+2$

The smallest number representable in two octets is -32768 itself, which is:

10000000 00000000

while the largest is $2^{15}-1$ (32767), which is:

01111111 11111111

In representing integer values, the minimum number of octets possible must be used. Putting this another way, the most significant nine bits of the contents must not all be the same (either all 1s or all 0s), as such a value could be represented by (at least) one fewer octet.

Thus, given the following definition:

v INTEGER ::= -27066

the value **v** is encoded thus:

02 02 9646_{16}

and can *not* be encoded as, for example:

02 04 FFFF9646

6.5.2   Real

The encoding of a real value is primitive, with the contents octets representing the value in one of four ways:

i)   the absence of contents octets (the value **0**);

ii)   assigned values of the first (and only) contents octet (the special values **PLUS-INFINITY** and **MINUS-INFINITY**);

iii) a binary representation, base 2, 8, or 16;

iv)   a character-based decimal representation.

Thus, the value **reallyZero**, defined as follows::

    reallyZero REAL ::= 0

is encoded as:

    09 | 00 |₁₆

In ii)-iv), the first octet is crucial in identifying which representation is being used, and conveying some parameters of it.

For the value **PLUS-INFINITY**, the single contents octet is as follows:

$$8\ 7\ 6\ 5\ 4\ 3\ 2\ 1$$
$$\boxed{0\ 1\ 0\ 0\ 0\ 0\ 0\ 0}$$
$$1$$

while for **MINUS-INFINITY**, it is:

$$8\ 7\ 6\ 5\ 4\ 3\ 2\ 1$$
$$\boxed{0\ 1\ 0\ 0\ 0\ 0\ 0\ 1}$$
$$1$$

Thus, the value **alephNull**, defined as follows:

    alephNull REAL ::= PLUS-INFINITY

is encoded as:

    09 | 01 | 40₁₆

The use of the binary representation is indicated by bit 8 of the first octet being set to 1. The remaining bits of the contents encode the value. There are actually five fields involved: the sign (S), the base (B), the binary scaling factor (F), the exponent (E) and a value N which is derived from the mantissa.

The first four of these are encoded using one of the following four possibilities, depending on the format of E. (N occupies all further octets, as determined by the overall length of the encoding):

```
8 7 6 5 4 3 2 1  8 7 6 5 4 3 2 1
1 S B B F F 0 0  E E E E E E E E
      1                2
```

```
8 7 6 5 4 3 2 1  8 7 6 5 4 3 2 1  8 7 6 5 4 3 2 1
1 S B B F F 0 1  E E E E E E E E  E E E E E E E E
      1                2                3
```

```
8 7 6 5 4 3 2 1  8 7 6 5 4 3 2 1  8 7 6 5 4 3 2 1  8 7 6 5 4 3 2 1
1 S B B F F 1 0  E E E E E E E E  E E E E E E E E  E E E E E E E E
      1                2                3                4
```

```
8 7 6 5 4 3 2 1  8 7 6 5 4 3 2 1  8 7 6 5 4 3 2 1       8 7 6 5 4 3 2 1
1 S B B F F 1 1   0 < n ≤ 255     E E E E E E E E   •   E E E E E E E E
      1                2                3                   n + 2
```

The various fields in the first octet have the following meanings:

bit 7	SIGN (S)	bit 6 5	BASE (B)	bit 4 3	Scaling factor (F)
0	+1	0 0	2	0 0	0
1	-1	0 1	8	0 1	1
		1 0	16	1 0	2
		1 1	reserved	1 1	3

The overall value so represented is:

$$S \times N \times 2^F \times B^E$$

where the first three factors constitute the mantissa. The purpose of the scaling factor (F) is to avoid the encoder having to shift the mantissa so that its least significant bit is on an octet boundary. It is only needed with the base 8 and 16 representations.

For example, the value **e**, defined as follows:

> **e REAL ::= {2918189707, 2, -26}**

can be encoded as:

$$09 \mid 06 \mid 80E60ADF0A8B_{16}$$

As can be seen from the diagrams, the exponent can be up to 255 octets in length. With an exponent of that size, it matters little whether N is 1 or takes the maximum possible number (10^{313}

approx.) of octets! The largest real number which can be represented is:

$$(2^{(2^{1010}-265)}-1) \times 2^3 \times 16^{(2^{2040}-1)}$$

which is approximately:

$$2^{2^{2044}}$$

Needless to say, this enormous number is a theoretical limit and the practical limits would of course be a lot less. Apparently the people who work with enormous numbers tend to use decimal representations anyway.

It is important to note that this real number representation is not based upon anything used in current floating-point hardware. This is because, despite the fact that there are standards in this area (IEEE Std 754-1985 and IEC Publication 559), there are still many different formats in use on different machines. In any event, the BER representation was designed to make it computationally inexpensive to convert into from any existing format. It is also easy to reverse the process, should the decoder use the same native format as the encoder. The effort of conversion, if the encoder and decoder use different native formats, is incurred by the latter.

Contrast this with an early proposal, which was to use the IEEE/IEC standard representation. Here, sending between two identical machines which do not use the standard internally would require two computationally expensive conversions with the attendant possibility of loss of precision.

There is no explicit indication of precision with the BER encoding. A broad indication is given by the size of the mantissa. However, if in some application it is important that the precision be indicated, then this would have to be done using a separate field of the protocol.

The decimal representation is indicated by bits 8 and 7 of the first octet both being 0. With this representation, the second and subsequent octets of the contents contain essentially ASCII characters, forming a field as specified in ISO 6093. Within this field, the value is represented using one of the representations of ISO 6093.

The representation to be used is indicated in the remainder of the first octet, as follows:

bit 6 5 4 3 2 1	Number representation
0 0 0 0 0 1	ISO 6093 NR1 form
0 0 0 0 1 0	ISO 6093 NR2 form
0 0 0 0 1 1	ISO 6093 NR3 form
0 0 0 1 0 0	
–	*reserved*
1 1 1 1 1 1	

6.5.3 Null

The encoding of a null value is primitive. Because there is only one value, no contents octets are required (or, indeed, permitted).

Thus, the value **NULL** of type **NULL** is encoded as follows:

05 | 00 |$_{16}$

6.5.4 Boolean

The encoding of a Boolean value is primitive. The contents part is a single octet, which contains the value 0 0 0 0 0 0 0 0 for **FALSE**, any other value, chosen by the encoder, for **TRUE**.

Thus, the value **TRUE** of type **BOOLEAN** can be encoded as follows:

01 | 01 | FF$_{16}$

or

01 | 01 | 01$_{16}$

and there are 253 other possibilities.

As a matter of interest, there are several other situations in the BER leading to multiple encodings representing the same value. (The multiple possibilities for encoding of values of the real type, as described above, gives another example). This makes the BER unsuitable for any purpose which requires the comparison of encodings to establish whether or not they represent the same value. One such purpose is in the validation of digital signatures. This has inspired a constrained version of the BER, called the distinguished encoding rules, where for each value there is only one possible encoding. This is described further in Chapter 9.

6.5.5 Enumerated

The encoding of an enumerated value is primitive. Except for the tag, the encoding is as for the integer value which represents it.

Thus, given the definition:

```
Priority ::= ENUMERATED {low(-1), medium(0), high(1)}
```

the value **low** of type **Priority** would be encoded as follows:

$0A \boxed{01} FF_{16}$

6.5.6 Bit, octet, and character strings

The encoding of values of string types may be either primitive or constructed at the choice of the encoder.

In a primitive encoding of a string, the octets simply represent the elements of the string (except that in a bit string encoding, the first octet is used to indicate how many unused bits there are in the last).

The characters of a character string are represented using the encodings inherent in the definition of that type of string. Depending on the type, certain control and graphic character sets are assumed to be invoked at the start of the string, and certain escape sequences assumed or permitted.

Given the definitions:

```
mask BIT STRING ::= '001110111011'B
os3 OCTET STRING ::= '0AE1C'H
pangram IA5String ::= "Veldt jynx grimps waqf zho buck"
```

the value **mask** can be encoded:

$03 \boxed{03} 043BB0_{16}$

the value **os3** can be encoded:

$04 \boxed{03} 0AE1C0_{16}$

and the value **pangram** can be encoded:

$16 \boxed{1F}$
$56656C6474206A796E78206772696D707320_{16}$
$77617166207A686F206275636B_{16}$

In a constructed encoding of a string, the nested encodings are themselves encodings of string values, and each represents a **segment** of the overall string. The lengths of and boundaries between the segments are chosen by the encoder and have no semantic significance. The overall string can be recovered by concatenating the elements from each segment, in order. The primary purpose of allowing segmentation of strings is to allow indefinite length encoding, such as would be needed if the start of a string were to be sent before its actual length was known.

The segments of a bit string are themselves bit strings, while the segments of octet *and character strings* are octet strings. The recursion implied there is indeed permitted; thus a segment may itself be segmented, to any depth.

It's *as if* ASN.1 contained the definitions:

BIT STRING ::=	[UNIVERSAL 3] IMPLICIT SEQUENCE OF BIT STRING
OCTET STRING ::=	[UNIVERSAL 4] IMPLICIT SEQUENCE OF OCTET STRING
IA5String ::=	[UNIVERSAL 22] IMPLICIT SEQUENCE OF OCTET STRING
...	

(which of course it does not, not least because these are built-in, not defined types).

In any case, as an example, consider the following value:

```
story IA5String ::=
     "Once upon a time  ..(800 chars omitted).. happily ever after."
```

The value **story** can be represented by the following primitive encoding:

$16 \boxed{82\,03\,45}_{16}$

$\qquad 4F6E63652075706F6E20612074696D65_{16}$

$\qquad 20...20_{16}$

$\qquad 68617070696C79206576657220616667465722E_{16}$

The same value can be represented by a constructed encoding, for example:

$36 \boxed{80}_{16}$

$\qquad 04 \boxed{11} 4F6E63652075706F6E20612074696D6520_{16}$

$\qquad \cdots$

$\qquad 04 \boxed{14} 68617070696C7920657665722061667465722E20_{16}$

$\qquad 00 \boxed{00}_{16}$

which uses the indefinite length variant. Notice the following points:

* the initial octet (the identifier) is different, because the form bit is now 1 for constructed;
* the segments have identifier 04_{16} for octet string;
* the end-of-constructor marker is present, because of the indefinite length.

The use of definite length for segmented strings is not actually precluded, it's just not particularly useful.

6.5.7 Object identifier

The encoding of an object identifier value is primitive. The contents consists of the packed sequence of numbers representing the arc labels. The packing is important, as it is expected that object identifiers will be carried frequently. Furthermore, as with tag numbers in the multiple octet variant of the identifier (see 6.2 above), it is not necessary for the receiver to retrieve the actual arc labels at run-time, only to be able to compare two object identifiers for equality. This can be achieved by comparing the packed representations.

In fact the similarity with tags in the identifier goes a bit further. Each number (except for the first two, which are combined into one) is represented as a series of octets, with 7 bits being used from each octet and the most significant bit being set to 1 in all but the last octet. The fewest possible number of octets must be used.

The contents is then simply the concatenation in order of the various series of octets.

The first two numbers, m and n, say, are combined into the single number $40m + n$. This saves an octet from every value, exploiting the fact that $0 \leq m \leq 2$, and that, except possibly for $m=2$ (joint-iso-ccitt), n is a very small number.

For example, given the following definition:

weatherReporting OBJECT IDENTIFIER ::= {2 6 6 247 1}

the value **weatherReporting** is encoded as:

06	05	5606817701$_{16}$

The contents here consists of representations of the four numbers 86, 6, 247, and 1 packed together. Each occupies a single octet (with the most significant bit set to 0) except for 247 which requires two octets (of which the second and last has the most significant bit set to 0).

6.5.8 Set, sequence, set-of, and sequence-of types

The encoding for a value of one of these structured types is constructed, and contains a nested encoding for each component value. In the case of sequence types, the component values must appear in the definition order. In sequence-of types, the order is meaningful, and must be preserved. In values of the set and set-of types, the component values may appear in any order convenient to the encoder.

For example, given the definitions:

TypA ::= SET{ p BOOLEAN,q INTEGER, r BIT STRING}
valA TypA ::= {p TRUE, r '83F'H, q -7}

the value **valA** can be encoded as any of the following (with many other possibilities besides):

$11|0B|_{16}$ $11|0B|_{16}$ $11|80|_{16}$

$01|01|01_{16}$ $03|03|0483F0_{16}$ $01|01|01_{16}$

$03|03|0483F0_{16}$ $02|01|F9_{16}$ $03|03|0483F0_{16}$

$02|01|F9_{16}$ $01|01|01_{16}$ $02|01|F9_{16}$

                                         $00|00|_{16}$

As a further example, given the definitions:

```
Readings ::= SEQUENCE OF INTEGER (-100..60)
medicineHat Readings ::=
            {-5,-4,4,15,20,24,29,28,20,15,3,-2}
```

the value **medicineHat** can be encoded as:

$10|24|_{16}$

$02|01|FB\ 02|01|FC\ 02|01|04\ 02|01|0F\ 02|01|14\ 02|01|18_{16}$

$02|01|1D\ 02|01|1C\ 02|01|14\ 02|01|0F\ 02|01|03\ 02|01|FE_{16}$

The only encoding variation allowed is in the choice of length variant.

6.5.9 Choice types

The encoding of a choice value is precisely that of the chosen alternative. Thus, given:

```
OneOrSeveralIntegers ::= CHOICE
{
    one      INTEGER,
    several  SEQUENCE OF INTEGER
}
```

the value **one -129** of type **OneOrSeveralIntegers** is encoded as:

$02|02|FF7F_{16}$

while the value **several {-129,0}** of the same type can be encoded as:

$10|07|\ 02|02|FF7F\ 02|01|00_{16}$

This is why protocols can be extended by replacing some type with a choice of that type and some others. Such an extension is backwards-compatible, that is, the systems developed to the old specification continue to conform to the new (at least syntactically). The one situation where this does not work is when the original type was implicitly tagged, as described in 4.2.6 above.

6.5.10 Any

The encoding of an any value is precisely that of the selected value of the selected type. Thus, the value **INTEGER -129** of type **ANY** is encoded as:

02 | 02 | $FF7F_{16}$

6.5.11 Tagged types

The encoding of a value of a tagged type is best described in terms of some encoding of the corresponding value of the base type. This is referred to as the **base encoding**.

Where the tagging is implicit, the encoding is the same as the base encoding, except that the tag (class and number) in the identifier part is replaced by the tag being applied. The form, length, and contents are as for the base encoding

Where the tagging is explicit, the identifier also reflects the new tag. However the encoding is always constructed, with exactly one nested encoding, the base encoding. This means that both tags are actually carried in the encoding

Consider the example of the value **-27066** of type **INTEGER**, whose encoding we showed above, as:

02 | 02 | 9646_{16}

The value **-27066** of type **[5] IMPLICIT INTEGER** is then encoded as follows:

85 | 02 | 9646_{16}

The encoding is the same except for the identifier, in which the tag class is now context-specific and the number is 5. Similarly, the value **-27066** of type **[APPLICATION 35] IMPLICIT INTEGER** is encoded as:

5F1F | 02 | 9646_{16}

The value **-27066** of type **[5] INTEGER** (assuming explicit tags as the default) is however encoded as:

A5 | 04 | 02 | 02 | 9646_{16}

Here the base encoding is found nested within the encoding. However the outer encoding has the new tag, of context-specific class, number 5. Notice, however, that the identifier is $A5_{16}$, rather than 85_{16} as it was for the implicitly tagged example. That is because the base encoding happened to be primitive, and with implicit tagging the form is preserved. With explicit tagging, however, the form is always constructed.

The value **-27066** of type **[APPLICATION 35] INTEGER** is encoded as:

7F1F $\boxed{04}$ 02 $\boxed{02}$ 9646$_{16}$

With implicit tagging and when the base encoding is constructed, it is only the outermost identifier whose tag is replaced. For example, given the value **'0001020304050607'H** of type **[0] IMPLICIT OCTET STRING**, a valid base encoding would be:

24 $\boxed{80}$ $_{16}$

    04 $\boxed{05}$ 0001020304$_{16}$

    04 $\boxed{03}$ 050607$_{16}$

    00 $\boxed{00}$ $_{16}$

and the corresponding encoding of the value would be:

A0 $\boxed{80}$ $_{16}$

    04 $\boxed{05}$ 0001020304$_{16}$

    04 $\boxed{03}$ 050607$_{16}$

    00 $\boxed{00}$ $_{16}$

The inner tags of octet string (universal class, number 4), for the segments, remain intact.

6.5.12 Useful and other defined types

The rules for the encoding of values of a defined type are just those which apply for the type which was assigned.

7 The Role of ASN.1 in OSI

This chapter overviews some of the important concepts of OSI, and describes the important role that ASN.1 plays in the upper layers.

7.1 Overview of OSI

Open Systems Interconnection (OSI) is an international project to standardise the way in which computers and other information processing systems communicate with one another. The foundation of OSI is the reference model, which, as is now well-known, divides the problem of inter-system communication into seven layers, each devoted to one aspect of the problem. Each layer builds upon the services provided by those below it to create a more powerful capability. This involves cooperation between the active objects within a layer (the layer entities) this being governed by a layer protocol.

A very significant layer boundary in OSI is that which separates layers 4 and 5. The lower layers (1-4), below that boundary, are concerned with provision of a data transfer service between the parts of a distributed application. The upper layers (5-7), above the boundary, are concerned with the cooperation among these various parts in pursuit of the application's goals.

This boundary, the transport-service, thus allows for separation of the concerns of communications technology and distributed application design. A particular network, say, can be used by many different applications; conversely, a particular application can operate over many different network types.

There are actually two types of service provided by the transport layer. The connection-oriented (CO) service is concerned with the establishment, use, and termination of transport connections. The use of such a connection allows the transfer, in either or both directions and subject to flow control, of data units, each containing an arbitrary number of octets. An expedited data capability may also be provided. The other service, the connectionless (CL) service provides for the transfer of data units without the need to establish a connection first. Here, each data unit contains a number of octets not exceeding a pre-defined maximum size.

The upper layers are: the Session Layer (layer 5), which is concerned with dialogue structuring; the Presentation Layer (layer

6), which is concerned with information representation; and the Application Layer (layer 7), which is concerned with everything else.

The nature of the Presentation Layer makes it the central focus as far as the role of ASN.1 goes, and its capabilities are therefore described in more detail (7.2) below. Nonetheless, ASN.1 is by no means a "part" of the Presentation Layer, as some accounts would have it. In fact, abstract syntaxes must be known by both Presentation and Application layers. The role of ASN.1 is described in 7.3.

The layering above transport was actually decided before any attempt to design a real application using it. This has led to a number of problems. For example, the purpose of putting dialogue structuring capabilities in the Session Layer was to factor out a set of mechanisms common to many or all applications. However, because the mechanisms were designed before the requirements of a significant number of applications were known in detail, the capabilities provided often seem ill-fitting, and an obstacle, rather than a help, to application design. By being in a single layer, the capabilities cannot be used in a nested or recursive fashion. Implementors often feel obliged to implement the whole thing, although some capabilities, or combinations of capabilities, are likely never to be needed.

A number of problems and issues with the upper layers, particularly the Presentation Layer, have been brought into focus by the existence and use of ASN.1. Some of these are briefly introduced in 7.4 below.

7.2   OSI Presentation Layer

The job of the Presentation Layer is to decide how information to be conveyed between its users (application-entities) is actually to be represented in transit. It also provides for the resulting encodings to be labelled, so that the receiving system can apply the appropriate decoding procedures.

The central core of this task is the maintenance of a collection of **presentation contexts**. A particular presentation context is an association between a particular known abstract syntax (such as that which provides the PDUs of a certain protocol) and a transfer syntax suitable for representing its values.

A value can only be sent if it belongs to the abstract syntax of some presentation context. When sent it is encoded using the corresponding transfer syntax. The identifier of the chosen presentation context accompanies the data, allowing them to be decoded.

This of course demands that the same presentation contexts are known to both presentation entities. In fact, associated with each presentation connection is a **defined context set** (DCS) containing zero or more presentation contexts. The initial DCS is negotiated during presentation connection establishment. There are optional presentation services which allow the DCS to be altered later, by the addition or deletion of presentation contexts (context management), and to be restored to a known state in the event of resynchronization (context restoration).

A presentation context is established by means of the following negotiation, usually carried out for several contexts in parallel.

The establishment of the context is requested by one presentation-user, which tells its local presentation-entity using the appropriate service primitive. The requestor determines and indicates the abstract syntax to be used. (A presentation context can be seen as a specific use of a particular abstract syntax. There can be more than one such use active concurrently, leading to multiple contexts with the same abstract syntax).

The presentation-entity local to the requestor then informs its peer (by means of the presentation-protocol) that a context is to be established, and lists one or more candidate transfer syntaxes that it is prepared to use. If the remote presentation-entity supports one or more of the candidate transfer syntaxes then it chooses one. If it does not then the context cannot be established.

The remote presentation-entity informs the remote presentation-user that a context is to be established, and tells it which abstract syntax is involved. The user has the chance to refuse the context, notwithstanding that a suitable transfer syntax was found.

The response is then conveyed back to the local presentation-entity, again by means of the presentation-protocol. If the context was successfully established, there is also an indication of which of the transfer syntaxes was chosen. The local presentation-entity tells the requestor whether the context was established or not. If it was established successfully, the context is considered part of the DCS.

Each presentation connection can also have an associated "default context" which must be used with certain presentation services and when the DCS is empty.

There are many presentation service primitives which have the capability of conveying "user data". Most important, perhaps is the primitive principally devoted to the task, P-DATA. The user data associated with each such primitive consists of a sequence of **presentation data values** (PDVs) from one or several presentation contexts.

The structure of the user data can be shown by means of the ASN.1 which describes it in the presentation protocol specification (the PDUs of the presentation protocol are defined using ASN.1 and, mostly, encoded using BER):

```
User-data ::= CHOICE
    {
        [APPLICATION 0] IMPLICIT Simply-encoded-data,
        [APPLICATION 1] IMPLICIT Fully-encoded-data
    }
```

This provides two possibilities for encoding. **Simply-encoded-data** is used when there is only one presentation context and therefore no need to signal to which context a particular PDV belongs.

```
Simply-encoded-data ::= OCTET STRING
```

Here the encodings of the various PDVs are simply concatenated together to form the contents of the octet string. (In fact, in some situations, this is optimised still further, with the octets being sent directly, rather than in a BER-encoded octet string).

Fully-encoded-data is used whenever there are (or might be) multiple contexts.

```
Fully-encoded-data ::= SEQUENCE OF PDV-list
PDV-list ::= SEQUENCE
{
    Transfer-syntax-name OPTIONAL,
    Presentation-context-identifier,
    presentation-data-values CHOICE
    {
        single-ASN1-type     [0]  ANY,
        octet-aligned        [1]  IMPLICIT OCTET STRING,
        arbitrary            [2]  IMPLICIT BIT STRING
    }
}
```

Each **PDV-list** contains one or more PDVs from the same presentation context. There is special treatment for the case where there is a single PDV belonging to a **single-ASN1-type** and it is encoded according to the BER (this avoids an extra level of encoding in that commonly-occurring case). Where these requirements are not met, but the encodings of the PDVs are each an integral number of octets, then the **octet-aligned** option is used. If even this is not met then the **arbitrary** option must be used.

If allowed by the applicable abstract syntax, it is possible for a PDV from a presentation context to carry PDVs from other presentation contexts embedded within it. The location of such embedded PDVs, and of course their interpretation, is governed by the (embedding) abstract syntax.

7.3   The role of ASN.1

ASN.1 is a notation for specifying data types and values of these types. Accordingly, its potential role in OSI is very broad, being usable for defining protocols at any layer. Notwithstanding this, ASN.1's prime use has been in the definition of application protocols. There are a number of reasons for this, but the dominant one is that almost all OSI protocols below the application layer were defined before ASN.1 was available. The one major exception to this, the presentation protocol, does in fact use ASN.1.

Were ASN.1 to have been available earlier, it is not out of the question that some of the other OSI protocols would have been defined using it. A number of examples in Chapter 4 above suggest that the OSI transport protocol could quite comfortably have been defined that way. Of course, it is much less likely that the BER would have been selected in those situations, as it would be rather too extravagant in octets for the lower layers.

Among the other reasons for the Application Layer being the prime area of use for ASN.1 is that the strengths of a notation for abstract syntax definition, as opposed to the use of *ad hoc* methods, are most apparent when the information involved is structured in a complex way. This is most likely to arise in application protocols.

The name which was chosen, *Abstract Syntax* Notation One, has led some to believe that it is intended only for the specification of abstract syntaxes in the narrow OSI sense described in 7.2 above, namely collections of application-significant data values for which the Presentation Layer negotiates encodings. While not in fact so restricted, this usage is indeed dominant.

Here the designer uses the notation to specify one or more abstract syntaxes, each being the values of a single ASN.1 type (commonly a choice type). The design of that ASN.1 type is of course a major part of the creative process involved. For example, the abstract syntax of the FTAM protocol (PCI) consists of the values of the type **PDU**, defined (here suitably abbreviated) as follows:

```
PDU ::= CHOICE
{
     f-initialize-request     [0]    F-INITIALIZE-request,
     ...,
     f-restart-response       [40]   F-RESTART-response
}
```

The definitions of all of these 41 PDUs go on to occupy 12 pages (over 700 lines) of notation.

Each abstract syntax is given a name (an object identifier value) which distinguishes it from all other abstract syntaxes in OSI. For example, the FTAM PCI abstract syntax is:

```
{iso standard 8571 abstract-syntax (2) ftam-pci (1)}
```

Having defined an abstract syntax as the values of an ASN.1 type, the definition of a suitable transfer syntax is then trivial. It is simply necessary to cite the application of the BER. It is not even necessary to give the resulting transfer syntax a name (object identifier) since that assigned to the BER itself can be used, namely:

```
{joint-iso-ccitt asn1 (1) basic-encoding (1)}
```

In fact, the implementation of this particular transfer syntax is commonly made a conformance requirement for OSI standards. There is nothing to prevent other transfer syntaxes from being implemented, and indeed they are and will be. The Presentation Layer sorts out which is to be used when the presentation context is established. However, having a single transfer syntax which every system can support promotes open interworking.

In sending PDVs from such an abstract syntax, there are a number of possibilities for the sending presentation-entity.

If the default context is used, or if the DCS contains only one context (and context management is not available) then the PDVs are "simply-encoded". Here the encoding of the PDV is simply sent as a string of octets by means of the session service. If more than one PDV is being sent, then the encodings are concatenated.

If the PDVs are not "simply-encoded" then they must be "fully-encoded". Here a value of the type **Fully-encoded-data** as described in 7.2 above is sent, encoded according to BER. The resulting encoding is sent as a string of octets by means of the session service.

To send a single PDV, whose encoding obeys the BER, the **single-ASN1-type** option of **Fully-encoded-data** can be used. The resulting string of octets might be as follows:

10 $\boxed{80}$ $_{16}$	{fully-encoded-data}
10 $\boxed{80}$ $_{16}$	{PDV-list}
02 $\boxed{01}$ 0A$_{16}$	{presentation context identifier: 10}
A0 $\boxed{80}$ $_{16}$	{single-ASN1-type}
id $\boxed{len}$ $contents$	{any value}
00 $\boxed{00}$ $_{16}$	
00 $\boxed{00}$ $_{16}$	
00 $\boxed{00}$ $_{16}$	

If multiple such PDVs are being sent, whether from the same or different presentation contexts, then several PDV-lists can be sent, each containing one PDV, thus:

$10\ \boxed{80}\ _{16}$	{fully-encoded-data}
$\quad 10\ \boxed{80}\ _{16}$	{PDV-list}
$\qquad 02\ \boxed{01}\ 0A_{16}$	{presentation context identifier: 10}
$\qquad A0\ \boxed{80}\ _{16}$	{single-ASN1-type}
$\qquad\quad id\ \boxed{len}\ contents$	{any value}
$\qquad\qquad 00\ \boxed{00}\ _{16}$	
$\qquad 00\ \boxed{00}\ _{16}$	
$\quad 10\ \boxed{80}\ _{16}$	{PDV-list}
$\qquad 02\ \boxed{01}\ 07_{16}$	{presentation context identifier: 7}
$\qquad A0\ \boxed{80}\ _{16}$	{single-ASN1-type}
$\qquad\quad id\ \boxed{len}\ contents$	{any value}
$\qquad\qquad 00\ \boxed{00}\ _{16}$	
$\qquad 00\ \boxed{00}\ _{16}$	
$00\ \boxed{00}\ _{16}$	

If a single PDV is being sent, but BER is not being used, then the value of **Fully-encoded-data** would instead be something like:

$10\ \boxed{80}\ _{16}$	{fully-encoded-data}
$\quad 10\ \boxed{80}\ _{16}$	{PDV-list}
$\qquad 02\ \boxed{01}\ 0A_{16}$	{presentation context identifier}
$\qquad 81\ \boxed{len}\ contents\ _{16}$	{octet-aligned}
$\qquad 00\ \boxed{00}\ _{16}$	
$00\ \boxed{00}\ _{16}$	

where this time an octet string value represents the encoded form of the PDV. If several PDVs from this same presentation context are being sent at the same time, then this same approach can be used, whether or not BER is involved, with the various encodings concatenated together within the octet string.

With an abstract syntax defined using ASN.1, the embedding of a PDV from some other presentation context is straightforward. All that is necessary is for the abstract syntax to include the type **EXTERNAL**. Each value of such a type is a PDV from an arbitrary presentation context, with the **indirect-reference** component indicating the presentation context involved.

7.4   Problems and issues

The X.409 notation (now ASN.1) and the OSI Presentation Layer
were developed in parallel, and on a rather different philosophical
basis. X.409 was an attempt to define and promote a single notation
and encoding scheme for high-level protocols. The Presentation Layer
takes a very primitive view of application information, and focuses
most of its efforts on accommodating diversity of encoding schemes.

Despite this inauspicious start, the pair have made a fairly
reasonable marriage. The presentation protocol is decribed in ASN.1,
and is (mostly) encoded using BER. ASN.1 provides the only
standardised way of embedding presentation data values. The
Presentation Layer provides some special support for abstract
syntaxes defined using ASN.1. Almost all OSI applications use
ASN.1 and BER together with the Presentation Layer, and they
work.

However, there are still a number of areas of dissonance. Most of
these are presently under discussion within the standards groups,
and will doubtless be resolved. A number of the problems and issues
are briefly sketched here, but without rigorous analysis or solutions.

7.4.1   Support for distributed applications

The concern of the Presentation Layer is the information conveyed
between two application-entities over a presentation connection, its
job being to negotiate the representation of such information. This is
fine for some of the "traditional" OSI applications like FTAM, which
are fully-defined in terms of such a pair of application-entities.
However, in some *distributed* applications the two application-
entities concerned in a particular presentation connection are by no
means the whole story. In X.400 Message Handling for example,
they may just be relaying a message which originated in some third
process and whose destination might be yet another.

In such a set-up, the relaying processes do not even know what
kind of information they are sending, and certainly can not take part
in sensible negotiations about its representation. Furthermore, the
actual sender and receiver processes do not even know each others'
identity, cannot communicate directly, and certainly do not have the
opportunity to negotiate.

Arguably, this situation could be accommodated by describing the
information to be relayed as an octet string. The information is
encoded by the sender and decoded by the receiver (within the
application layer) and the relaying systems do not have to worry
about it.

Similar, but perhaps better, is the use of **EXTERNAL** with **direct-reference**. Here the encoding, which may still be in the form of an octet string, is accompanied by an object identifier which tells the receiver what it is. However, because of the overhead, this is only practical if the information to be relayed is in one piece (or relatively few pieces). For example, this is the case for the message contents in X.400.

However, neither of these approaches work if the information to be relayed is not clearly separated from the rest of the information being carried. In X.400, for example, each process does not know whether the next is simply a relay or whether it will actually need to process the information. In the OSI Directory standard (X.500) names made up of attributes are used to determine the routing of a request. However a process does not know which attributes the next process will need to understand.

This situation, arguably complex enough, is made more complex by the problem of evolution of the protocols, and the consequence that the different processes involved do not all understand the entire message. Several of the other issues following are also related to this topic.

7.4.2 Structured abstract syntaxes and encoding rules

As mentioned above, the Presentation Layer was defined using some fairly primitive assumptions about application information. This is not altogether a bad thing and certainly provides a lot of flexibility to the designer. However it means that certain things that seem very natural in ASN.1 are not accommodated properly.

From the Presentation Layer's point of view, an abstract syntax is simply a set of PDVs, and a transfer syntax is just a mapping between PDVs and encodings. No structure is involved, except that embedded PDVs are envisaged.

In contrast, consider the (very simple) abstract syntax defined by the values of type **AS** as follows:

```
AS ::= CHOICE
{
      pdu1      [0]  PDU1,
      pdu2      [1]  PDU2
}
PDU1 ::= SEQUENCE
{
      a             INTEGER (0..2),
      b             BOOLEAN
}
PDU2 ::= ENUMERATED {v1(0), v2(1)}
```

This abstract syntax contains precisely eight PDVs, which can be written down using value notation as follows:

```
pdu1 {a 0, b TRUE}
pdu1 {a 1, b TRUE}
pdu1 {a 2, b TRUE}
pdu1 {a 0, b FALSE}
pdu1 {a 1, b FALSE}
pdu1 {a 2, b FALSE}
pdu2 v1
pdu2 v2
```

As far as the Presentation Layer it is completely irrelevant that there is structure here. Perfectly acceptable transfer syntaxes for this abstract syntax would just allocate different bit patterns to these eight PDVs. Here are just two examples:

PDV	transfer syntax 1	transfer syntax 2
pdu1 {a 0, b TRUE}	'111'B	'010'B
pdu1 {a 1, b TRUE}	'11111'B	'101'B
pdu1 {a 2, b TRUE}	'11'B	'000'B
pdu1 {a 0, b FALSE}	'1111111'B	'011'B
pdu1 {a 1, b FALSE}	'1111'B	'111'B
pdu1 {a 2, b FALSE}	'1'B	'100'B
pdu2 v1	'11111111'B	'001'B
pdu2 v	'111111'B	'110'B

Now clearly this situation should not be precluded. However it could be argued that there are many advantages with structured abstract syntaxes, as provided for by the use of ASN.1. These advantages are reinforced if the transfer syntax is not "hand-carved" as with those above, but mechanically derived by the application of encoding rules. The Presentation Layer does not recognise the existence of encoding rules *per se*, only the transfer syntaxes which derive from them.

The advantage of encoding rules such as the BER is that the structure of the abstract syntax is preserved in the encoding. This makes it possible to evolve protocols, and to generate sensible errors for values out of range (see the discussion of "exceptions" below).

Many ways can be imagined in which **AS** above could be evolved. New PDU types could be added, for example, or new components added to the existing PDUs. With an encoding rule approach, these changes can be accommodated without having to redesign the transfer syntax. Furthermore, values which are outside of the abstract syntax (at least as far as one process is concerned) may be partially understood.

7.4.3 Exceptions and the scope of ASN.1

The Presentation Layer is defined to abort the presentation connection if it finds some encoding which does not correspond to a value in the abstract syntax. What if the abstract syntax is defined using ASN.1, and somewhere, deep in some PDU definition, is the following:

```
...
INTEGER (0..100)
...
```

If some structure-preserving encoding rules such as BER are used, then the case where the value **101** is actually sent can be distinguished from all other error cases. Possibly the application would like to be able to reply with a specific "out of range" error. However, this is not possible, because according to the present model, the PDU will never even reach the Application Layer. In fact the first it will know is when the Presentation Layer "pulls the plug" on the connection.

Thus it could be argued that the abstract syntax definition should have just read:

```
...
INTEGER
...
```

then any integer would be acceptable to the Presentation Layer, and the application would be free to signal as many error cases as it sees fit. Here, however, the user of ASN.1 is just limited to expressing the set of values which the Presentation Layer will not abort the connection over, rather than expressing the true application intent.

It has been suggested that one way out of this is to recognise that there are actually two abstract syntax concepts, one which circumscribes the Presentation Layer's behaviour and one which describes the values which the application layer regards as correct. ASN.1 could then be used for both of these, the latter perhaps being expressed as a subtype of the former.

This raises a further point, however. If an ASN.1 definition used in an abstract syntax specification says:

```
X ::= SEQUENCE
{
    a    INTEGER OPTIONAL,
    b    REAL OPTIONAL
} -- at least one of a and b must be present
```

does the comment actually form part of the abstract syntax definition in the sense that the presentation connection would be aborted if the value {} were sent? Or should the designer be forced to say:

```
X
(
    WITH COMPONENTS {...,a PRESENT}
|   WITH COMPONENTS {...,b PRESENT}
)
```

if such a constraint is intended to form part of the abstract syntax?

7.4.4   ANY

When the **ANY** "type" was included in X.409 it seemed perfectly natural, and furthermore to be a clear requirement. What it meant, in essence, is that one level of protocol did not care what the actual type was which governed some field. Some other level of protocol would worry about that. All that was necessary was that the outer-level should be able to skip over it, and the encoding rules made sure of that. When, later on, it was known what was actually supposed to be in that field, perhaps after some application processing had already taken place, then it could be interpreted.

This *mañana* approach to PDU interpretation does not sit well with the Presentation Layer approach. Conceptually, the Presentation Layer must be able to decode the PDU completely into some value from the abstract syntax. How could decoding take place iteratively, with application layer knowledge influencing the process, especially given the Presentation Layer view that encodings, and even PDVs, are unstructured?

(This is not an implementation problem but a modelling one. OSI does not constrain implementors to build systems in any particular way, and certainly does not require them to structure their software according to layers, although many have done so).

The problem is that an ASN.1 specification containing **ANY** alone is not a complete specification of an abstract syntax in OSI terms.

This problem produced a rather half-baked attempt at solution, namely **ANY DEFINED BY**. The idea was that, by including in the abstract syntax specification an indication of how the actual type of the any value could be obtained, it would make things respectable as far as the Presentation Layer was concerned. However, **ANY DEFINED BY** is not nearly flexible enough. It also raises the question of exceptions as mentioned above. If the value indicated is not one of those which the presentation-entity knows about, or if, after the determination, the any value turns out to be of the wrong type, does this lead to the presentation-connection being aborted? In most uses of **ANY**, this would certainly not be the intent.

8 Implementation Matters

Software tools which implement various aspects of ASN.1 and BER are available, and are virtually a necessity for developing OSI application protocols. This chapter briefly explores what it means to implement ASN.1 and/or BER, and thus what such tools comprise.

8.1 Overview

ASN.1, by allowing protocol information to be specified using a formal language, provides scope for partially automating protocol development. A useful analogy, introduced at the start of this book, is the high-level programming language. Just as the programming language hides details of storage layout, address lengths and formats, and number representation, which previously were the concern of the programmer, so ASN.1 hides details of encoding which previously had to be the concern of the protocol designer.

The programming language analogy is also a valuable one when it comes to implementation of ASN.1. There are a collection of activities which can be classed as "compile-time". There can in principle be a whole development environment, involving ASN.1 compilers, perhaps for different target environments, editors, libraries, syntax checkers, pretty printers. The ultimate purpose of this is to create object code which executes at "run-time", that is, when the communications governed by the relevant protocol is actually taking place. In this case, the object code is not the executable form of some arbitrary program, but is the encoding and decoding software, tailored to the particular abstract syntax and transfer syntax involved.

This can be depicted as follows:

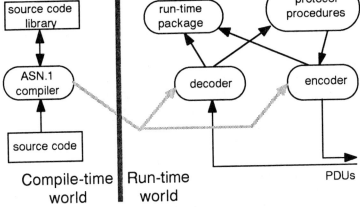

The lines representing showing the encoder and decoder as outputs of the compiler are shown differently to represent the shift to the run-time environment.

8.2 Compile-time

The task of ASN.1 compilation is essentially to take, as input, text files which purport to obey the syntax of ASN.1, to check that they do, and, if so, to produce encoders and/or decoders to be used in the running system.

We might speculate that the compilation process could be organised into a front-end and a back-end. The former would be concerned with the parsing (recognition) of the language, and the transformation of the ASN.1 source into a convenient internal data structure. The latter would be concerned with production of object code to exist in the run-time environment. The back-end is closely tied in with the nature of the object code, various possibilities for which are sketched in 8.3 below. We will thus restrict ourselves for the time being to consideration of the front-end, the parser.

There are a number of aspects of ASN.1 which make its parsing particularly difficult, though not, with the possible exception of some pathological macros, impossible. As described in Chapter 9 a number of changes are being considered to the language which will alleviate some of these difficulties.

ASN.1 modules can have mutual cross-references. There is not, therefore, a certain order in which a collection of modules can be processed such that definitions can be found before they are used. This hinders separate compilation of modules. Of course the problem of use before definition is found even within one module. This requires either multi-pass techniques, or strategies for making assumptions on as-yet-undefined names, the assumptions to be checked later on in the process.

Unfortunately, the nature of some of the ASN.1 constructs means that chains of mutually-dependent assumptions have to be created in some cases. The constructs involved, and an example, are described in 9.1. The most severe problem here is that there are situations in which it is not even possible to recognise where one assignment statement ends and another begins until a definition is later encountered which settles the matter.

The worst problem by far, however, is the macro capability. With certain fairly simple restrictions on its generality, it can be processed successfully, and there are ASN.1 compilers which can do so. The restrictions would have to prevent the macro designer from including strings like "::=" in the new notation.

The following macro "eats" the rest of any unfortunate module in which it is used, stopping only when encountering a fellow macro:

```
VORACIOUS MACRO ::=
BEGIN
TYPE NOTATION ::= Eat
VALUE NOTATION ::= empty
Eat ::= "END"  -- belch -- | "MACRO"  -- pass --  | EatSomething Eat
EatSomething ::= type | identifier | number | Keyword | Special
Keyword ::=   "NULL" | "TRUE " | "FALSE" |
              "PLUS-INFINITY" | "MINUS-INFINITY"
Special ::=   "::=" | "," | "{" | "}" | "." | "(" | ")"
              "" string "B" |
              "" string "H" | """ string """
END
```

A more substantial difficulty with macros is that usually the intent is not satisfied simply by the parsing of the type and value notation. Instead the intent of the macro designer is typically that some meaning be ascribed to the information which the macro user actually supplied. For example, in the case of the ROS **OPERATION** macro, the intent is to introduce a relationship between a particular operation code and a particular argument data type (among others). This relationship is then used as the basis for resolving an **ANY DEFINED BY** in the ROS protocol. Thus, some kind of table needs to be produced as a result of parsing the macro instances, a table which can later be used in some protocol implementation. Unfortunately, there is no general-purpose way in which this can be done at present, so special code has to be written for each macro.

These are among the reasons why there are plans to replace macros, as described in 9.2.

Most ASN.1 compilers require directives to be included in the source module to guide some aspects of the compilation process. Some employ special comments, such as those starting "--*", for directives, whereas others allow directives to appear in certain syntactic contexts.

The kinds of guidance that might be provided by directives are:

- whether the encoder, or the decoder, or both, is to be capable of handling some type. This reflects the fact that many abstract syntaxes are actually asymmetrical, with each party in the communication needing only to be able to generate certain PDVs, and not to recognise them;
- which form of length is to be used for encoding values of some type. Sometimes the encoder is set up to make the decision based upon the size of the value, in which case a directive indicating the maximum size for primitive encodings may be necessary;
- the amount of space needed for some string, and whether static or dynamic memory allocation is to take place.

Other directives may be concerned with optimising in different ways the operation of the encoder or decoder.

8.3   Run-time

The purpose of ASN.1 run-time software is to allow its users (typically application protocol machines) to create, send, receive, and interpret encoded ASN.1 data values.

To do so, of course, the ASN.1 run-time has to coexist harmoniously with the software concerned with communicating the encoded values or coordinating that communication. This is completely dependent on the architecture of the overall implementation, and protocol stack, and is in any case not really germane to this book. We will focus here on the encoding and decoding task, and the communication of that information to the users.

Looking at the second of those first, we find two general strategies which could be adopted.

One, perhaps that which is most often employed, involves providing the user with a subroutine and a data structure declaration (in some programming language, typically "C") for each data type whose values are to be encoded or decoded. These constitute the object code produced by the compiler.

On input, the user calls the appropriate subroutine, which, if the received octets are valid, decodes them into the form described by the data structure declaration. To further access the information, the user simply uses the relevant programming language constructs to access the various components of the received value.

To output, the user formats a data area according to the data structure declaration, and calls the relevant subroutine, passing the data as parameter. The result is that the data are encoded using the appropriate encoding rules and then sent.

The second strategy involves providing the user with subroutines for accessing the various components of encoded values. If the received value is a set, for example, the user will be provided with subroutines to read particular component values.

Which of these strategies is more effective and efficient will depend on the nature of the application.

All of the subroutines provided are likely to be built using a run-time package including the low-level routines which create or pick apart encodings. In the case of BER, for example, there might be encoding routines for setting tag values, length fields, and to create the contents for various kinds of primitive values; and decoding routines for reading these various things from a received PDU.

The compiler-generated subroutines may be built directly in terms of the low-level ones. Alternatively, they may be generic routines driven by compiler-generated tables. Such a table may hold, in a convenient form for processing, the type information from the ASN.1 description, for example as follows:

next	points to the next component if this type is appearing in a structure
optionality	indicates whether it is a mandatory or optional component
type	indicates which built-in type this is, or points to another type table if a multiply-used defined type
default	if defined, points to the default value
tags	points to the start of the list of tags
subtypes	points to the start of the list of subtype specifications
type-dependent	information specific to the built-in type. For example, in a structured type, this might point to the first of the component types

Besides the type table, certain other tables will be required, including those for tags, values and subtype specifications.

For example, given:

```
X ::= SET
{
    a    INTEGER (0..255),
    b    BOOLEAN DEFAULT TRUE,
    c    SEQUENCE OF OCTET STRING
}
```

the compiler may create tables something like the following:

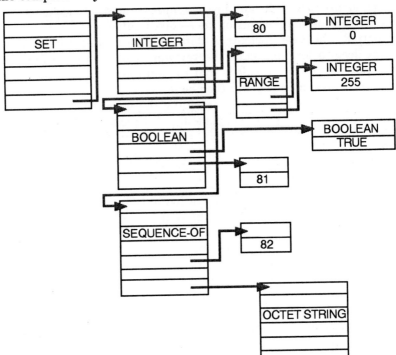

There are many challenging design aspects to the ASN.1 run-time and encoders and decoders. Many are concerned with efficiency of processor and storage utilisation. This is not important at compile-time. Any work which can be done at compile-time instead of run-time should be. For example, the identifier in the BER encoding, can with the possible exception of the form bit, be generated at compile-time, with no run-time processing of the tag class and number. A similar argument applies to the object identifier encoding.

Among the important considerations are:

- memory management, given the need to handle incoming encodings of arbitrary size;
- handling of large encodings without unnecessary copying;
- strategy for handling BER length fields, given that the length, which itself is a variable number of octets, occurs before the contents which it describes, and must include the lengths of all the components. One well-known technique is to generate the PDU backwards, allowing the length to be added only after it is already known.

9 Future Development of ASN.1

At the time of writing (summer 1990) work is under way on a programme of enhancement to ASN.1. Whenever possible, backwards compatibility with the present notation will be maintained. The work, being carried out collaboratively by CCITT and JTC1, is expected to produce revised standards in around 1992. This chapter introduces the various areas presently being explored for enhancement. In no case has a final decision to make the change been taken.

9.1 Fixing defects

The specifications of ASN.1 and BER involve a large number of concepts, described in a large number of closely-spaced pages of text, with a high information density. Accordingly, it is inevitable that a number of errors and ambiguities will be found. The group with responsibility for ASN.1 have started a "defect handling" activity, which involves receiving, reviewing, and processing reports of defects. Any changes, other than the most trivial, to fix the defects are balloted to ensure that they are internationally acceptable.

A number of defect reports are already in process, and balloting is already under way on the one which is perhaps the most dramatic. The defect (or group of related defects) has been well known for several years, but hitherto has been regarded as an irritant rather than a fatal flaw. However, as part of a general cleaning-up exercise, it has been decided to seek approval to fix it.

The defect is that some of the notational constructs make the machine parsing of the language unnecessarily difficult. The basic problem is that the (assignment) statements of the language are not separated or terminated, so it is not always clear when type or value notation is expected. This in turn would be no problem if all type and value notation were properly delimited and distinguishable.

However some of the constructs are problematic in that regard:

- the abbreviations **SET** (for **SET OF ANY**) and **SEQUENCE** (for **SEQUENCE OF ANY**), which lead to type notation being a leading substring of other type notation. This would be fine were it not for ...

- the **ANY** value notation, a leading substring of which is valid type notation;
- the choice value notation, which, with nested choices, can have an arbitrary number of identifiers followed by an actual value. However ...
- value references look like identifiers;
- anything can be used before it is defined.

(To say nothing about macros, with their completely arbitrary notation, particularly value notation).

This means that to parse an ASN.1 module properly, an arbitrary look-ahead may be needed. Consider the following string which a parser may encounter:

```
...   a B :: = c d E :: = F g H :: =   ...
```

If **B** turns out to be a choice type and **c d** a choice value, we get an interpretation:

```
...   a B :: = c d
      E :: = F
      g H :: =  ...
```

If **c** is assumed to be a defined value, **E** can be interpreted as an any type and **F g** as an any value. Thus, we get an interpretation:

```
...   a B :: = c
      d E :: = F g
      H :: =    ...
```

The intended solution to this is three-fold:

i)   add ";" as a terminator to all assignment statements;
ii) change the **ANY** value notation to include a colon ":" between its two parts;
iii) eliminate the abbreviations **SET** and **SEQUENCE**.

The problem is that the changes are (to say the least) not backwards-compatible and it may be judged that they should not be made. The first of these may seem the most drastic but in fact even if a module is published without colons it would be very easy for a human to put them in, using the layout to show the ends of the statements, something which the machine is not entitled to assume.

It is not expected that there will be further changes (as opposed to additions) of this magnitude.

The problem mentioned above was actually discovered by people developing parsers for the language. A number of other areas of deficiency in the specification have been discovered by parser developers, who actually have to program the rules of the language and soon uncover any slackness. The two most significant are probably scope rules and type compatibility.

The scope rules of a language are concerned with the use of names, particularly the multiple use of names with different meanings in different contexts. It turns out that the rules of ASN.1 are not so clear as they should be in this regard. For example, given:

```
ModA DEFINITIONS ::=
BEGIN
      TypeA         ::=  INTEGER {idA(0)}
      idA TypeA     ::=  1
      TypeB         ::=  SEQUENCE
                         {
                              i       TypeA DEFAULT idA
                         }
END
```

it turns out to be unclear from the specification whether the default value of component i of **TypeB** is the integer value **0** or **1**.

An attempt is presently being made to write a complete and precise specification of the scope rules of ASN.1.

The main question of type compatibility can be depicted thus:

```
      v1 T1 ::= ...
      v2 T2 ::= v1
```

where T1 and T2 are both type notation (the place of the ellipsis must of course be taken by some value notation, but its form is not really important here). T1 and T2 are said to be **value assignment compatible** if this is valid. But given two pieces of type notation, when are they compatible in this way ? It turns out, once again, that the specification is not entirely clear on the matter, and work is being done to make it so.

9.2   Macro replacement

In many ways the most unsatisfactory aspect of ASN.1 as it is now is the macro capability. It is unsatisfactory, not because it is unnecessary (although some would hold this view), or because of the difficulty in understanding the specification (which is considerable), or because of the bugs which have been found there (which are relatively trivial). These aspects have however fuelled a continuing controversy about the capability. In my view, it is unsatisfactory because it does not go far enough in solving the problem it was designed to address.

In any case, one of the ASN.1 enhancements currently planned is the replacement of macros with something better. (Macros would probably be retained for some period, allowing their existing users to migrate to the replacement, then phased out).

Recall from Chapter 5 above that the macro capability was originally added in 1983 to support the **OPERATION** concept which CCITT had earlier intended to add to X.409 as a built-in type. In fact, **OPERATION** turns out to have been just the first of many concepts fitting the same general pattern: many of these have led to the definition of macros.

The general pattern is as follows:

A one specification defines a new kind of information object, and specifies the general properties that such things have
e.g. the operation concept in the Remote Operations (ROS) standard

B users of the specification can design their own specific instances of that information object
e.g. their own specific operations

C the specification must leave appropriately shaped "holes" in its protocol to carry information unique to particular instances
e.g. the ROS protocol must be able to invoke an operation regardless of the data type of its argument

D each particular instance may induce a "linkage" between fields in the protocol
e.g. if an operation code field indicates that the operation is "submit message", the corresponding argument field must be of type "message"

ASN.1 presently supports **C** (through **ANY**) and part of **D** (through **ANY DEFINED BY**). The macro capability, however, can do a partial job of meeting **A** (by macro definition) and **B** (by application of the resulting macro) and this has encouraged its use.

The aim of the project presently aimed at macro replacement has the aim of satisfying **A-D** in a coordinated manner. As a matter of fact, it is quite likely that as a result of the work, not only macros but another somewhat unsatisfactory aspect of ASN.1, **ANY** (including **ANY DEFINED BY**) can also be phased out. (The underlying capability, to have fields in PDUs which are open-ended with regard to type, will of course need to be retained).

The solution to macro replacement has been an elusive one, with a number of proposals having been submitted. None of these has, at the time of writing, received universal approval from the committee.

However, there seems to be a consensus emerging that the solution will involve replacing macros with "tables". Where in the past a macro would be defined, instead a table type would be defined.

A table type governs the number of columns in the table, and their characteristics. The columns correspond to the various facets of this kind of information object. For example, in the **OPERATION** table one column might be declared to hold object identifier values; this might model the opcode of the operation. Another column might be declared to hold arbitrary ASN.1 types; this might model the argument of the operation. The capability to define table types meets **A** above.

A different user can then define particular rows of such a table, corresponding to particular instances of that kind of information object. The row of the **OPERATION** table corresponding to the "submit message" operation for example, could be defined by supplying a specific object identifier value for the opcode column, and a specific data type ("message") for the argument column. As well as individual rows, a user can also define, name, export and import rowsets. The capability to define rows and row-sets meets **B** above.

The designer of the protocol can define PDUs to depend on the contents of various rows of various tables. This meets **C** and **D**.

The present Working Document also proposes, as part of the overall solution, the addition of functions and "@"-expressions to ASN.1.

Functions are expressions which must be supplied with appropriate parameters before they can be used as complete types (or values). They have a wide range of uses but most notably allow abstract syntaxes to be partially-defined, the complete definition only being available when some row-set of a particular table has been supplied.

"@"-expressions (pronounced "at") allow the value of one component of a structure (such as a set or sequence) to depend on the value of another. They can be seen in some ways as a generalisation of **ANY DEFINED BY**.

9.3 Character strings

Another less than satisfactory feature of ASN.1 is its treatment of character strings. ASN.1 presently has eight different character string types. Some are too limited in their repertoire (**NumericString**, **PrintableString**, even **IA5String**) particularly for international applications. Some are rather too general (**GraphicString**, **GeneralString**); no implementation can handle all character sets and neither of these types gives any hint of what its values might contain. Some people would say there are too many types (should I choose **T61String** or **GraphicString** for my international application?); some ask for more (please add a type corresponding to ISO 8859).

To be fair, the confusion in ASN.1 is to some extent a direct reflection of confusion in character set standardisation itself.

In any case an attempt is now being made to rationalise the situation. An important objective is to permit the character sets required for a particular application to be specified more precisely than by use of **GraphicString** or **GeneralString**, and more flexibly than by modification of ASN.1 to introduce a new specialised type.

A catalyst in this is the progress in the character set standards committee towards the "ultimate" character set standard. This work will result in ISO 10646 (a number exactly 10000 more than that allocated to international ASCII) which is a 32-bit character set. (Thankfully, there are optimisations which mean that one would very rarely have to send 32 bits in practice). This standard contains within it alphabets from all over the world, together with symbols needed in specialised areas, such as mathematics, the programming language APL and even the International Phonetic Alphabet.

The way ahead is likely to be the introduction of a single new character string type, based upon ISO 10646, and which can be used to unify ASN.1's treatment of character strings. This will also have the following beneficial properties:

- the existing character string types of ASN.1 can be redefined as subtypes of the new type (but with the encoding rules defined to achieve backwards compatibility);

- ISO 10646 allows the definition of the notion of abstract character. This has been a bit difficult to pin down so far in ASN.1. While the unit of measure of character strings for the purpose of subtyping is "the character" it turns out that this is not competely well-defined;

- ISO 10646 provides names for around 6000 characters, and several standard repertoires and sub-repertoires. These can form the basis of more comprehensive value and subtype notations for character strings. By defining an algorithm for deriving built-in value and type references from the names in ISO 10646, it will not be necessary for the ASN.1 document to replicate all of these, or to be updated when new characters are added.

This will provide comprehensive notational support for the specification of character sets. However, there is another vital piece to the whole solution. Frequently it will be desirable not to "hard-wire" into an abstract syntax definition the character sets to be used, but to negotiate them separately. It has been proposed that the Presentation Layer's negotiation mechanisms be used for this purpose.

The actual strings themselves will normally be carried embedded in data values from some abstract syntax. If separate negotiation is to occur for those strings this would require the use of **EXTERNAL** to carry the embedded PDVs, and indicate from which presentation context they come. However this may be found to be too heavyweight for use with character strings, adding several octets per string.

A variant under consideration is the introduction of a new notion, **character abstract syntax** (CAS), an abstract syntax in which the set of values are characters. A transfer syntax for a CAS would specify the encoding both for single characters and for strings of characters. In addition, there would be an alternative to **EXTERNAL** designed specifically to carry embedded PDVs from CASs (it may be called **EXTERNAL CHARACTER STRING** for example). As opposed to the ordinary **EXTERNAL**, such a container would be optimised for carrying character strings and would introduce minimal overhead, normally a single octet, in the encoding.

9.4 New encoding rules

Ever since the X.409 notation and encoding were separated, the former becoming ASN.1 and the latter its *basic* encoding rules, it has been envisaged that different encoding rules might be desirable under some circumstances. Certainly there are quite likely to be proprietary alternatives already, invented for various reasons, such as to achieve backwards compatibility with a pre-existing encoding style, to optimise the representation of values of some particular types, or to use 7-bit representation.

So far, however, no alternatives have been standardised. Mostly this is because the BER are quite adequate for a wide range of applications, and have certainly been good enough to allow the development and deployment of OSI products. There is also much to be said for having a single standard, used universally. For example, this allows it to be implemented once and used often.

Notwithstanding this, there is now work going on to define new standardised encoding rules for ASN.1. The motivation is not to provide general-purpose alternatives to the BER, but specialised alternatives, more suitable than the BER in some particular respect. It is likely that OSI applications will continue to require conforming implementations to support the BER; this will permit open interworking. The Presentation Layer negotiation mechanisms will allow other encoding rules to be negotiated.

There are three sets of encoding rules under development, all based upon BER: the packed encoding rules (PER), distinguished encoding rules (DER) and confidential encoding rules (CER). A proposal has also been made to standardise some "light-weight" encoding rules, although no decision has been taken to proceed.

Some work is also taking place on the "ground rules" for the definition of new encoding rules. This has already raised the question of extensibility. For example, with BER, the valid encodings of **value1**, defined thus:

```
value1 SEQUENCE
{
     a    INTEGER,
     b    INTEGER
}
::=
{
     a    5,
     b    10
}
```

and **value2**, defined thus:

```
value2 SEQUENCE
{
     a    INTEGER,
     c    BOOLEAN  OPTIONAL
     b    INTEGER
}
::=
{
     a    5,
     b    10
}
```

are identical, both being:

$$10 \boxed{06} 16$$
$$0\,2 \boxed{01} 05_{16}$$
$$0\,2 \boxed{01} 0A_{16}$$

This means that with BER, extra optional components can be added to sequences in a future version of an application protocol, and provided the protocol is defined so that new components are omitted when communicating with a process developed according to the old specification, the latter will notice no difference. This in turn means that such changes do not need to result in the allocation of a new abstract syntax name. Such a property of encoding rules could be called extensibility.

However, not all encoding rules are extensible in this way, which means that if the application designer wishes to have the freedom to make such changes, then there is a requirement that only extensible encoding rules are permitted.

The proposed packed encoding rules (PER) are not extensible. They are based upon BER, but exploit the fact that if sender and receiver are operating to exactly the same specification of the abstract syntax, then BER has some redundancy.

With PER, the redundant parts of the encoding are simply not sent. For example, in an encoding of **value1** above, BER includes two identifier octets carrying the tag for **INTEGER**. Neither of these is necessary, since the receiver is assumed to be expecting two integer components. With BER the length of the overall sequence would also be sent. This is also redundant, since the receiver knows that the end comes after the second integer value. Besides the removal of such redundancy, there may be some minor tweaking, such as not including an explicit length for integers.

Using PER, therefore, **value1** would be encoded thus:

10_{16}
$\quad 05_{16}$
$\quad 0A_{16}$

and **value2** thus:

10_{16}
$\quad 05_{16}$
$\quad 020A_{16}$

With **value1** five octets are saved over BER, and with **value2** four octets. The extra octet is needed in **value2** to indicate the presence of the second integer, rather than the Boolean, and therein lies the inextensibility.

As with PER, the distinguished encoding rules (DER) are based upon BER; however, instead of removing octets, they simply remove all options from the sender. The resulting encodings are thus also valid by BER.

Distinguished encoding rules are required for some security applications, most notably digital signatures. In fact, a set of such rules have already been internationally standardised, but for a specific application, the authentication framework of the OSI Directory. The DER will adopt these as the basis, but may make modifications to widen their applicability.

The need for a distinguished encoding derives from the nature of digital signatures. A digital signature is computed from a particular message, is sent along with the message and serves to provide some assurance of the latter's integrity. The receiver carries out the same computation as the sender and checks that the result is the same as that transmitted. (To ensure that false signatures cannot be generated, encipherment is also involved).

The key point is that the receiver must be able to reproduce exactly the same computation as the sender, given the same message. Since in OSI the same message may be represented differently at different times, at the decision of the Presentation

Layer, the use of the transmitted encoding is not an appropriate basis for the computation because false negative checks will occur. Even where the same transfer syntax is used (e.g that derived from BER), that is insufficient, because of the optionality. (As just one instance, in one situation a Boolean of value true may be represented by FF_{16} whereas in another it may be represented by 80_{16}).

Some set of encoding rules that produce encodings which are in one to one correspondence with the abstract values - *distinguished* encoding rules - are therefore needed. The work is using BER as the basis, and eliminating all of the sender's options.

There may be other security applications which require the elimination of sender's options. For example, the elimination of covert communication channels demands that redundant representations be eliminated to avoid their use being modulated to carry information.

The third new set of encoding rules being considered are the confidential encoding rules (CER), also connected with security, and also based upon BER. The idea here is to allow selective encipherment of parts of a transmitted value, with the decision to encipher or not being taken by the sender. The CER work by allowing a complete (I-L-C) encoding anywhere within the PDU to be replaced at the option of the sender by its enciphered form. The fact that this has happened is signalled by wrapping the enciphered form inside an **EXTERNAL** data value. Unlike the normal use of **EXTERNAL**, this does not appear in the notation. As it turns out, the adjective *confidential* is a bit of a misnomer here because the rules can be used for many other kinds of transformation besides encipherment.

9.5 Miscellaneous

There are a number of miscellaneous enhancements presently being considered.

The subtyping notation may be changed to allow some more flexibility in the combining of value sets. Presently it is possible to express an "or" (set union of value sets), and by concatenating subtype specifications, an "and" (set intersection). However it is presently not possible to use "not" (set difference) to exclude specific value sets. Nor is it possibly to combine "and", "or" and "not" in a flexible way. It is proposed to add these abilities.

Some new useful types are under consideration, including **Date**, to carry a date without time of day, and **ParameterisedIdentifier**, a combination of an object identifier value and parameter information.

ASN.1 Reference

Appendix A:
ASN.1 syntax (basic items)

A.1 ASN.1 character set

The following characters can be found in ASN.1 specifications:

A B C D E F G H I J K L M N O P Q R S T U V W X Y Z
a b c d e f g h i j k l m n o p q r s t u v w x y z
0 1 2 3 4 5 6 7 8 9 ( ) { } [ ] < > : ; = , . - ' "

Within two of the basic syntactic items which are described below, comment and cstring, additional characters can appear.

A.2 Basic syntactic items

The table below describes the basic syntactic items of ASN.1. Each item is shown as it appears in the syntax diagrams of Appendices B and C. A "string" is a sequence of zero or more characters, while a "name" is a string of at least one character, drawn from A-Z, a-z, 0-9 and hyphen ("-"). In a name a hyphen cannot appear as the last character or adjacent to another hyphen.

Syntactic item	Contains
bstring	string of 0s and 1s, bracketed by "'" and "'B"
comment	a pair of hyphens ("--") followed by a string of arbitrary characters and terminated by the end of a line or a pair of hyphens, whichever is first
cstring	string of characters from some ASN.1 character set, with """ represented by """"
hstring	string of hexadecimal digits (0-9, A-F) bracketed by "'" and "'H"
identifier	name starting with lower-case letter
modulereference	name starting with upper-case letter
number	one or more decimal digits; no leading zeros
typereference	name starting with upper-case letter
valuereference	name starting with lower-case letter

A number of additional basic items are added for macros:

(astring)	string of characters from the ASN.1 character set
(localtypereference)	name starting with upper-case letter
(localvaluereference)	name starting with *upper*-case[†] letter
(macroreference)	name in which all letters are upper-case
(productionreference)	name starting with upper-case letter

[†]   This is presently a discrepancy between the ISO and CCITT versions, the latter aligning this with value reference. The discrepancy seems to have originated in a misinterpretation of X.409, ASN.1's predecessor.

A.3 Non-alphabetic items

The brackets, separators, terminators and other special symbols of ASN.1 are as follows:

{	starts a list
}	ends a list
[	starts a tag
]	ends a tag
(	starts a subtype expression starts a named number, bit or object identifier component
)	ends a subtype expression ends a named number, bit or object identifier component
<	"alternative of" in selection type starts embedded definitions (macros)
>	ends embedded definitions (macros)
{...,}	starts a list in partial specification of inner subtyping
"	starts or ends character string value
,	separates list items
.	separates module reference from type or value reference
;	terminates import and export statements
..	range separator

Ⓘ	alternative subtype value set alternative syntax (macros)
⊖	(hyphen) minus sign for negative numbers
⊚(::=)	"defined as" in assignments (also for introducing module body and macro alternative list)
⓪	zero (exact real value)
②	indicates binary base for real value
⑩	indicates decimal base for real value

A.4 Keyword items

The following character sequences constitute the keywords of ASN.1. Unfortunately, as shown by the annotations, it is somewhat unclear which of these are reserved, that is, not available for for use in forming identifiers and references. Accordingly, it is recommended that all of the keywords should be avoided when forming such names.

ABSENT†	ANY	APPLICATION†	BEGIN
BIT	BOOLEAN	BY†	CHOICE
COMPONENT†	COMPONENTS	DEFAULT	DEFINED†
DEFINITIONS†	empty**	END	ENUMERATED†
EXPLICIT†	EXPORTS†	EXTERNAL	FALSE
FROM†	IA5String°	identifier**	IDENTIFIER
GeneralizedTime°	GeneralString°	GraphicString°	IMPLICIT
IMPORTS†	INCLUDES†	INTEGER	ISO646String°
MACRO*	MAX†	MIN†	MINUS-INFINITY†
NOTATION*	NULL	NumericString°	number**
OBJECT	ObjectDescriptor°	OCTET	OF
OPTIONAL	PLUS-INFINITY†	PRESENT†	PrintableString°
PRIVATE†	REAL†	SEQUENCE	SET
SIZE†	string**	STRING	TAGS†
TeletexString°	TRUE	type*	TYPE*
T61String°	value*	VALUE*	VideotexString°
VisibleString°	UNIVERSAL†	UTCTime°	WITH†

†   not reserved by ISO 8824, but reserved by CCITT X.208. This is not a deliberate difference but arose from misalignment of publication schedules.

*   reserved inside macro definitions.

**   can appear inside macro definitions, but not reserved.

°   character set type or useful type; it is not clear whether or not these are reserved (anomalously, EXTERNAL, a useful type, is reserved).

Appendix B:
ASN.1 syntax

The complete syntax of ASN.1, excluding the macro capability, is shown in the syntax diagrams which follow. The various diagrams, each named for the part of the syntax which they illustrate, are arranged in alphabetical order for easy reference.

An ASN.1 module is only valid if it corresponds to some path through the diagrams, starting with Module and following other diagrams whenever their names appear on the path. The path through a diagram must proceed from the start to the end and travel only in the direction of the arrows (never following a line "upstream").

Comments and white-space can freely appear between, but not within, syntactic items.

Each diagram is of the following form:

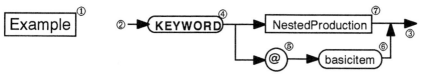

KEY

① the name of the part of the syntax being illustrated.
② the start of the path to be followed (always near the upper left corner).
③ the end of the path (almost always near the upper right corner).
④ a keyword of the syntax(A.4), shown in boldface within a rounded box.
⑤ a non-alphabetic item (A.3), shown within a circle or rounded box.
⑥ a basic item of the syntax (A.2), shown in a rounded box.
⑦ the name of a diagram which is logically nested within this one, shown in a rectangle.

In defining the syntax, these diagrams are not sufficient, because there are context-specific rules, such as that forbidding the multiple use of the same identifier within a set type, or insisting that the members of that set type have distinct tags. Such rules are described following the diagram of the affected construct.

Some rules constrain a Type to be "of integer type" (for example). In determining whether some Type is indeed appropriate in such a situation, it must be reduced to its associated BuiltInType, as described under "Type" below. It can then be said to be "of integer type" if and only if the resulting BuiltInType is IntegerType.

In this description, tagging is subsumed by the concept of Type. Thus the "tagged types" of the tutorial do not appear as such.

Further rules:

a) the **DEFINED BY** option can only be present in BuiltinType in Type in NamedType in ElementType in SetType (or SequenceType).

b) the identifier must be that of another component of the SetType (or SequenceType) and that component must be of integer or object identifier type.

Further rules:

a) Value must be a value of Type.

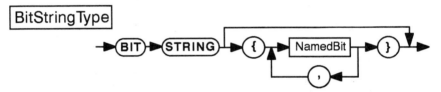

Further rules:

a) the significance of trailing zero bits is decided by the user and may be indicated by comment.

b) the identifiers in the various NamedBits must be distinct, as must the bit positions.

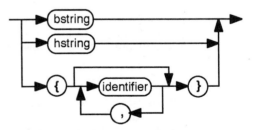

Further rules:

a) if trailing zero bits are significant then the notation starting "{" cannot be used, and the hstring notation can only be used if the value contains a multiple of four bits.

b) in the bstring and hstring notations, earlier digits correspond to lower-numbered bits.

c) in the hstring notation, each hexadecimal digit describes four bits, with the lower-numbered being more significant.

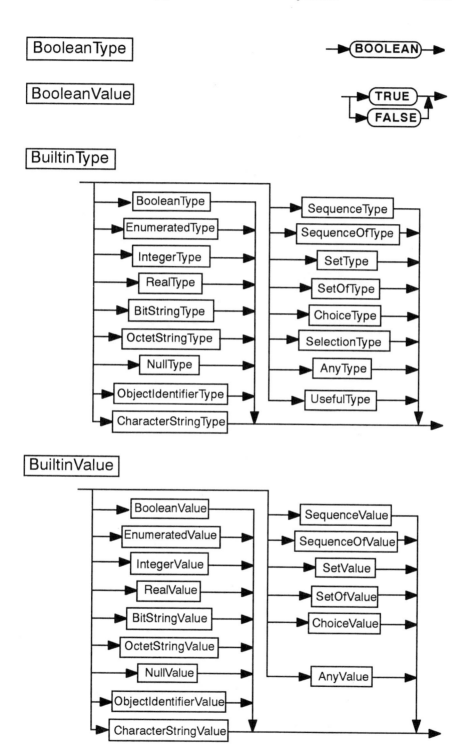

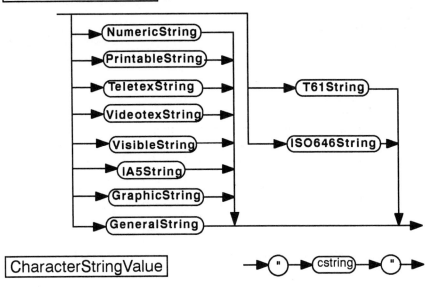

CharacterStringType

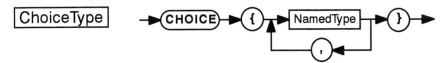

CharacterStringValue

Further rules:

a)   the characters in the cstring must all belong to the character set implied by the corresponding type.

ChoiceType

Further rules:

a)   the identifiers in the various NamedTypes must be distinct, as must the tags of the types.

b)   this type has the tags of all of the NamedTypes.

ChoiceValue

Further rules:

a)   if an identifier is present, Value must be a value of the identified alternative of the corresponding ChoiceType.

b)   if no identifier is present, Value must be a value of an alternative (of the corresponding ChoiceType) with no identifier.

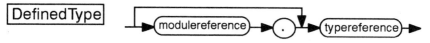

DefinedType

Further rules:

a) if no modulereference is present, the typereference must appear in a TypeAssignment, or (if not) as (precisely one) Symbol in Imports, in (the current) Module.
b) if a modulereference is present, then the typereference must appear in a TypeAssignment in (the identified) Module.
c) if Imports is present in (the current) Module, then the modulereference must appear in a ModuleIdentifier therein, and the typereference must be one of the Symbols imported hence.

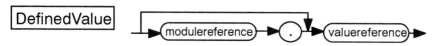

DefinedValue

Further rules:

(As for DefinedType, but replacing typereference by valuereference and TypeAssignment by ValueAssignment).

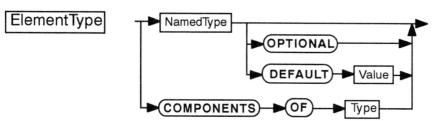

ElementType

Further rules:

a) the Value must be a value of the type of the NamedType.
b) the Type must be a set (sequence) type if this appears in a SetType (SequenceType).

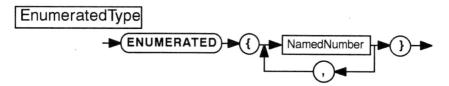

EnumeratedType

Further rules:

a) the identifiers in the various NamedNumbers must be distinct, as must the integer values.

EnumeratedValue

Further rules:

a) the identifier must be one of those appearing in the corresponding
EnumeratedType.

Exports

Further rules:

a) each Symbol must appear as the reference in an assignment
(type, value, or macro, as appropriate) in the current Module.

b) a particular Symbol cannot appear more than once.

Imports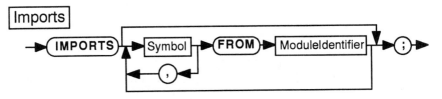

Further rules:

a) each Symbol must appear as the reference in an assignment
(type, value, or macro, as appropriate) in the Module identified by
the closest following ModuleIdentifier.

b) all Symbols imported from the same Module must appear in a
contiguous list (without an intervening ModuleIdentifier), and a
particular Symbol cannot appear more than once in such a list.

c) each ModuleIdentifier must appear as it does in the identified
Module, except that if an ObjectIdentifierValue is present then the
modulereference may be changed if it is necessary to allow
unambiguous reference (when the same Symbol is imported from
two Modules with the same modulereference).

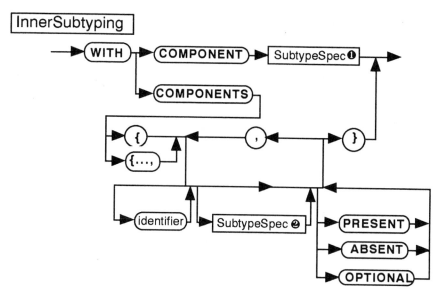

Further rules:

a) **WITH COMPONENT** is permitted only if the parent type is a set-of type or sequence-of type, and SubtypeSpec❶ must be a valid subtype specification for the component type.

b) the identifier, if present, must be one of those appearing in the parent type, and identifies the component to which any following constraint applies. If the identifier is omitted, then the constrained component is identified by position.

c) where the parent type is a set type or a sequence type, a constraint (though perhaps empty) must be present for every mandatory component.

d) SubtypeSpec❷ must be a valid subtype specification for the constrained component.

e) where the parent type is a set type or a sequence type, **PRESENT, ABSENT**, and **OPTIONAL** are only permitted if the constrained component is optional.

f) where the parent type is a choice type, **OPTIONAL** is not permitted.

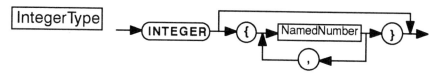

Further rules:

a) the identifiers in the various NamedNumbers (if any) must be distinct, as must the integer values.

 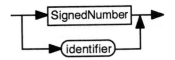

Further rules:

a) the identifier must be one of those appearing in the corresponding IntegerType.

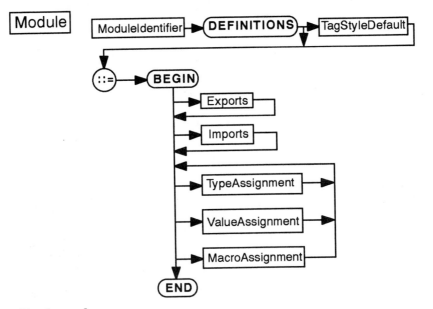

Further rules:

a) each Module should be assigned an ObjectIdentifierValue to appear in its ModuleIdentifier.

b) each assignment must have a distinct reference.

c) if no TagStyleDefault is present, explicit tagging is the default.

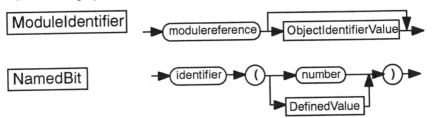

Further rules:

a) the DefinedValue must be of integer type, and must be non-negative.

b) the number or DefinedValue identifies a bit position (from zero).

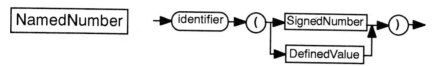

Further rules:

a) the DefinedValue must be of integer type.
b) the SignedNumber or DefinedValue provides an integer value.

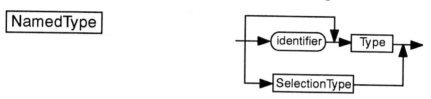

Further rules:

a) where a SelectionType is present, the identifier is considered to be
    that which appears therein, and the type is considered to be the
    appropriate alternative of the choice Type which appears therein.

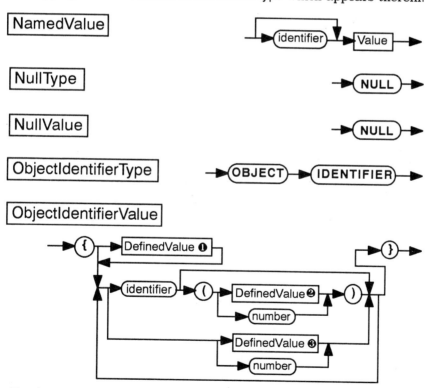

Further rules:

a) the DefinedValue❶ (if present) must be of object identifier type.

b) each DefinedValue❷ or DefinedValue❸ must be of integer type, and must be non-negative.
c) an identifer must be followed by "(", unless it is one of the predefined object identifier components shown in Appendix D.

Further rules:

a) if necessary, trailing zeros are deemed to have been added so that the string denotes an integral number of octets.
b) in the bstring notation, each successive group of eight bits denotes a successive octet of the value.
c) in the hstring notation, each successive pair of hexadecimal digits denotes a successive octet of the value. The first of the pair is more significant.

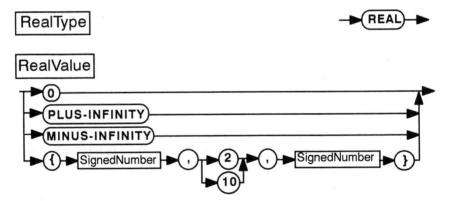

Further rules:

a) the notation containing the single item "0" is used if and only if the value is zero exactly.

Further rules:

a) the Type must be a choice type.

SequenceType

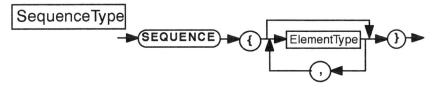

Further rules:

a) below, and in the further rules for SequenceValue, each ElementType which is a "**COMPONENTS OF**" is considered to have been replaced, *in situ*, by the elements of the designated sequence type. In the event of nested "**COMPONENTS OF**", this is applied repeatedly. This must be possible in a finite number of steps.
b) the identifiers in the various ElementTypes must be distinct.
c) each series of consecutive ElementTypes marked **OPTIONAL** or **DEFAULT** must have distinct tags from each other, and from the following ElementType, if there is one.

SequenceValue

Further rules:

a) there must be exactly one NamedValue for each ElementType in the corresponding SequenceType which is not marked **OPTIONAL** or **DEFAULT**, and zero or one for each which *is* so marked.
b) the NamedValues must appear in the order in which the ElementTypes appear in the corresponding SequenceType.
c) the element to which a NamedValue corresponds may be indicated by an identifier, which must appear in the corresponding SequenceType.

SequenceOfType

SequenceOfValue

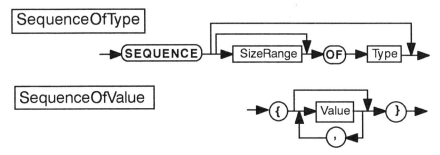

Further rules:

a) each Value must be of the Type which appears in the corresponding SequenceOfType.

SetType

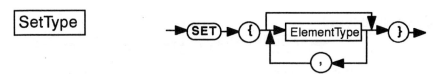

Further rules:

a) below, and in the further rules for SetValue, each ElementType which is a "**COMPONENTS OF**" is considered to have been replaced, *in situ,* by the elements of the designated set type. In the event of nested "**COMPONENTS OF**", this is applied repeatedly. This must be possible in a finite number of steps.

b) the identifiers in the various ElementTypes must be distinct, as must the tags of the types.

SetValue

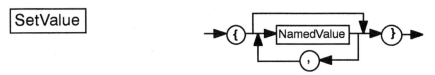

Further rules:

a) there must be exactly one NamedValue for each ElementType in the corresponding SetType which is not marked **OPTIONAL** or **DEFAULT**, and zero or one for each which *is* so marked.

b) the element to which a NamedValue corresponds may be indicated by an identifier, which must appear in the corresponding SetType.

SetOfType

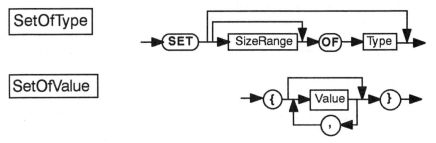

SetOfValue

SetOfValue image continued

Further rules:

a) each Value must be of the Type which appears in the corresponding SetOfType.

SignedNumber

SizeRange

Further rules:

a) the SubtypeSpec must be a valid subtype specification for **INTEGER (0..MAX)**.

SubtypeSpec

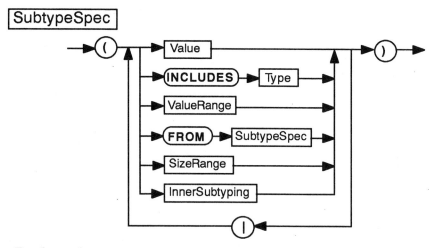

Further rules:

a) the valid subtype specifications for various parent types are shown in Appendix E below. Therein, the possibilities shown above by Value alone, **INCLUDES**, and **FROM** are referred to respectively as single value, contained subtype, and permitted alphabet.

b) Value must be a value of the parent type, as must Value❶ and Value❷ in SizeRange.

c) Type must be a subtype of the parent type.

d) SubtypeSpec must be a valid subtype specification for the same parent type, but of **SIZE(1)**.

Symbol

Tag

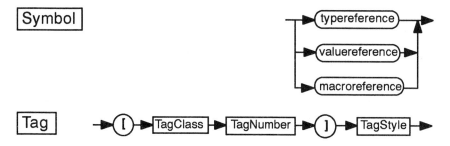

TagClass

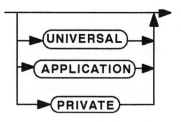

Further rules:

a) the **UNIVERSAL** option is only available to the designers of ASN.1 itself.

TagNumber

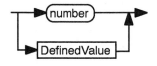

Further rules:

a) the DefinedValue must be of integer type, and must be non-negative.

TagStyle

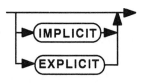

Further rules:

a) when neither **EXPLICIT** nor **IMPLICIT** is present, the TagStyle-Default for the current Module is taken.

TagStyleDefault

Type

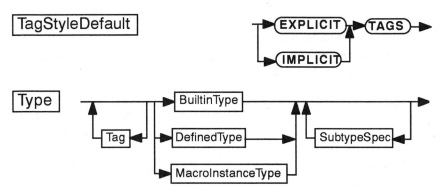

Further rules:

a) the last Tag must not include **IMPLICIT** if the BuiltinType or DefinedType is an (untagged) choice or any type.

b) the SubtypeSpecs must be valid for the BuiltinType or DefinedType. The valid subtype specifications for various parent types are shown in Appendix E below.

c) if the macro being instantiated by the MacroInstanceType can deliver different types for different MacroInstanceValues, then the rule (a) also applies here, and there must be no SubtypeSpecs.

d) where it is necessary to reduce a Type to its associated BuiltInType, this is done by iteratively discarding Tags and SubtypeSpecs, replacing any DefinedType by the Type by which it was defined, and reducing any MacroInstanceType to its delivered type.

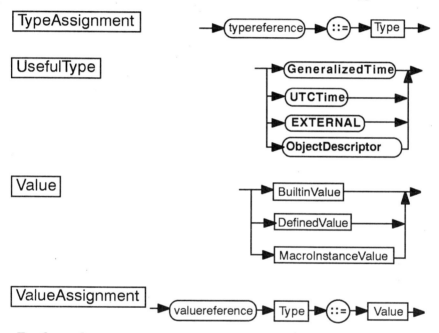

Further rules:

a) the Value must be a value of Type.

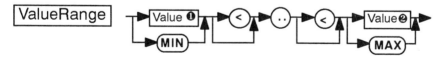

Further rules:

a) if both Values are present, then Value❶ must be not greater than Value❷.

Appendix C:
ASN.1 syntax (macros)

The syntax of the ASN.1 macro capability is shown in the syntax diagrams which follow. The various diagrams, each named for the part of the syntax which they illustrate, are arranged in alphabetical order for easy reference. They use the same style and rules as those in Appendix B above. There are three references into these diagrams from the main ASN.1 in Appendix B. They are:

    MacroAssignment
    MacroInstanceType
    MacroInstanceValue

corresponding, respectively, to the definition of a macro, its use in type notation, and its use in value notation.

EmbeddedDefinitions

147

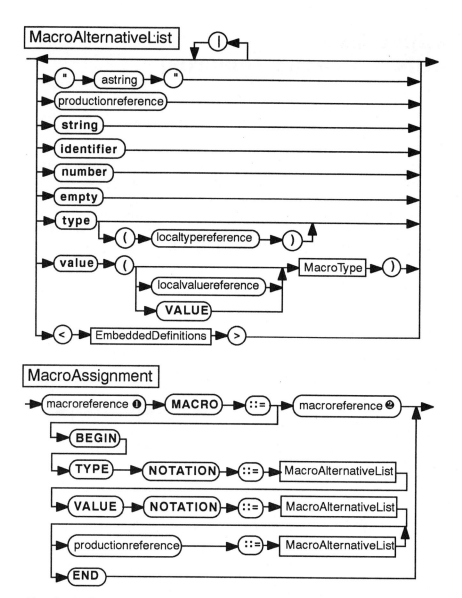

Further rules:

a) every productionreference appearing in a MacroAlternativeList must appear precisely once at the outer level of this construct.

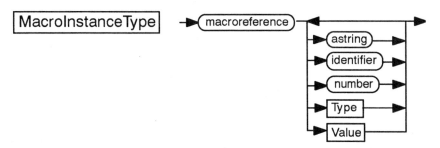

Further rules:

a) the sequence of items following the macroreference must obey the syntax of the type notation associated with that macroreference.

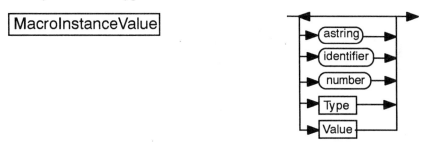

Further rules:

a) the sequence of items must obey the syntax of the value notation associated with the macro used to define the type of which this is a value.

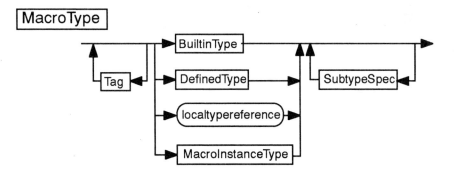

Further rules:

a) this is identical to Type, except that the additional alternative localtypereference has been added.

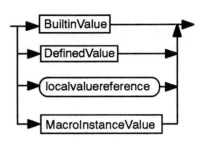

Further rules:

a) this is identical to Value, except that the additional alternative
localvaluereference has been added.

Appendix D:
The object identifier tree

The following diagram depicts the object identifier tree (OIT). The upper reaches, those defined within ASN.1 itself, are shown in their entirety. In addition, a number of examples are given.

To determine the object identifier components allocated to a particular node in the tree, it is necessary to follow the unique path from the upper left corner to the node, gathering the numbers encountered on the way.

The built-in symbolic identifiers provided (those which need not be followed by the number in parentheses) are shown in left side of the diagram. (They are in plain text, as opposed to the examples, which are in italics). They are supplemented with the 26 single letters of the alphabet (lower-case) which can be used for the arcs following {ccitt recommendation}, as with the example of c in the diagram.

The various examples shown in the diagram can be rendered in ASN.1 as follows:

CCITT Recommendation C.75 (fictional):
  {ccitt recommendation c 75}
CCITT Rapporteur Group on Directory Systems, 1985-88 :[32]
  {ccitt question 7 directorySystems(35)}
United Kingdom telecommunications administration:[33]
  {ccitt administration unitedKingdom(234)}
Telecom Canada:[33]
  {ccitt network-operator telecomCanada(3101)}
ISO FTAM protocol specification:
  {iso standard ftam(8571) part(4)}
European Computer Manufacturer's Association:
  {iso identified-organization icd-ecma(12)}
ASN.1 basic encoding rules (for use as a transfer syntax name):
  {joint-iso-ccitt asn1 (1) basic-encoding (1)}
"Surname" attribute in the ISO/CCITT OSI Directory standard
  {joint-iso-ccitt ds(5) attributeType(4) surname(4)}
D. Steedman, proud owner of X.400 (1988) T-shirt, number 247
  {joint-iso-ccitt mhs-motis(6) group(6) dSteedman(247)}

---

[32] The group didn't actually use this branch because it allocated its object identifiers jointly with ISO in another branch.

[33] There is no implication herein that this particular node is actively used for object identifier allocation.

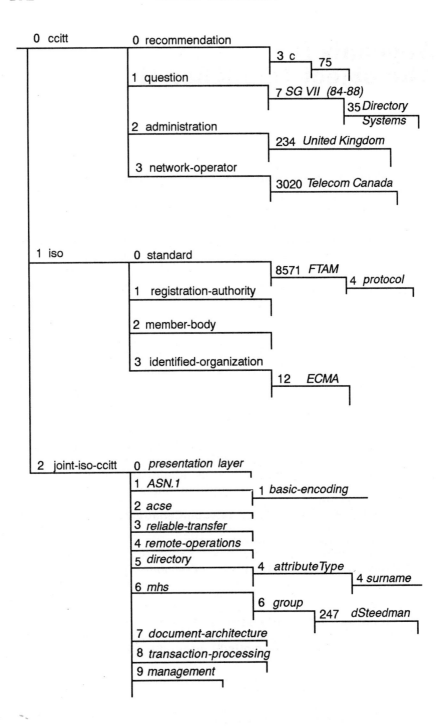

Appendix E:
Subtype value sets

The following table shows which of the various value set constructs are applicable for subtyping each built-in type. The same possibilities are then available for any type which has been derived from such a built-in type by tagging and/or subtyping.

The useful types and selection types have been omitted from the table. In the former case, the subtyping possibilities can be deduced from the definition of the type (see Appendix G). In the latter, the subtyping possibilities are precisely those of the selected alternative, whatever it may be.

Built-in type	single value	contained subtype	value range	size range	alphabet limitation	inner subtyping
BOOLEAN	✔	✔	✗	✗	✗	✗
INTEGER	✔	✔	✔	✗	✗	✗
ENUMERATED types	✔	✔	✗	✗	✗	✗
REAL	✔	✔	✔	✗	✗	✗
OBJECT IDENTIFIER	✔	✔	✗	✗	✗	✗
BIT STRING	✔	✔	✗	✔	✗	✗
NULL	✔	✔	✗	✗	✗	✗
OCTET STRING	✔	✔	✗	✔	✗	✗
character string types	✔	✔	✗	✔	✔	✗
SEQUENCE types	✔	✔	✗	✗	✗	✔
SEQUENCE OF types	✔	✔	✗	✔	✗	✔
SET types	✔	✔	✗	✗	✗	✔
SET OF types	✔	✔	✗	✔	✗	✔
ANY	✔	✔	✗	✗	✗	✗
CHOICE types	✔	✔	✗	✗	✗	✔

Appendix F:
Universal tag allocation

The allocation of tags of the universal class is as follows (tag numbers in decimal):

0	*reserved* (*)
1	**BOOLEAN**
2	**INTEGER**
3	**BIT STRING**
4	**OCTET STRING**
5	**NULL**
6	**OBJECT IDENTIFIER**
7	**ObjectDescriptor**
8	**EXTERNAL**
9	**REAL**
10	**ENUMERATED** types
11 - 15	*reserved*
16	**SEQUENCE** and **SEQUENCE OF** types
17	**SET** and **SET OF** types
18	**NumericString**
19	**PrintableString**
20	**TeletexString (T61String)**
21	**VideotexString**
22	**IA5String**
23	**UTCTime**
24	**GeneralizedTime**
25	**GraphicString**
26	**VisibleString (ISO646String)**
27	**GeneralString**
28 - +∞	*reserved*

(*) this tag number is used within the ASN.1 basic encoding rules to represent "end-of-contents marker", and thus will never be allocated to any future type.

155

Appendix G:
Definitions of the useful types

The definitions of the useful types of ASN.1 are shown below. For convenience, the definitions are contained in a module structure. However no such module appears in the standard, and it is not necessary (or indeed permitted) for a user to import the definitions explicitly in order to be able to use them.

```
ASN1UsefulTypes DEFINITIONS   IMPLICIT TAGS::=
BEGIN
    EXTERNAL ::=          [UNIVERSAL 8]   SEQUENCE
    {
        direct-reference       OBJECT IDENTIFIER OPTIONAL,
        indirect-reference     INTEGER OPTIONAL,
        data-value-descriptor ObjectDescriptor OPTIONAL,
        encoding               CHOICE
            {
                single-ASN1-type    [0]  ANY,
                octet-aligned       [1]  OCTET STRING,
                arbitrary           [2]  BIT STRING
            }
    }


    GeneralizedTime ::=   [UNIVERSAL 24]  VisibleString


    ObjectDescriptor ::=  [UNIVERSAL 7]   GraphicString


    UTCTime ::=           [UNIVERSAL 23]  VisibleString

END
```

List of abbreviations

ACT ONE	(an algebraic specification language)
ASCII	American Standard Code for Information Interchange
ASN.1	Abstract Syntax Notation One
BCD	binary coded decimal
BER	basic encoding rules
BNF	Backus-Naur form
CAS	character abstract syntax
CCITT	International Telegraph and Telephone Consultative Committee
CER	confidential encoding rules
CL	connectionless
CO	connection-oriented
DCS	defined context set
DER	distinguished encoding rules
FDT	formal description technique
FTAM	file transfer, access, and management
IEC	International Electrotechnical Commission
IEEE	Institute of Electrical and Electronics Engineers
I-L-C	identifier-length-contents
ISO	International Organization for Standardization
JTC1	Joint Technical Committee 1 (of ISO/IEC)
LOTOS	(a standardised FDT based on the temporal ordering of observational behaviour)
MDN	macro definition notation
MHS	message handling systems
OIT	object identifier tree
OSI	open systems interconnection
PCI	protocol control information
PDU	protocol data unit
PDV	presentation data value
PER	packed encoding rules
ROS	remote operations
TLV	type-length-value
TPDU	transport protocol data unit
UTC	universal coordinated time

Glossary of terms

abstract syntax: a named set of distinct values which can be communicated.

alphabet limitation: a form of value set, suitable for character strings, which includes those strings composed of some subset of the characters.

alternative: a component of a choice type.

any type: an unrestricted choice type, whose values are all of the values of all possible ASN.1 types, whether built-in or defined.

application-wide: a class of tag intended for types expected to be of common utility across a whole application protocol or protocol family.

base: the number, 2 or 10, which is raised to the power of the exponent in expressing a real value.

base encoding: relative to a value of some tagged type, the encoding of the corresponding value of the type without tagging.

bit string type: a built-in type whose values are the ordered sequences of bits (binary digits).

Boolean type: a built-in type with the two values true and false.

built-in type: a type provided directly by ASN.1.

C

character abstract syntax: (under consideration) an abstract syntax in which the values are characters.

character string type: a type whose values are ordered sequences of characters, drawn from some character set.

choice type: a structured type, defined in terms of a collection of distinct alternatives, each of whose values is a value of one of the alternatives.

component: one of the types in terms of which a structured type is defined.

constructed: a form of encoding in which the contents is a sequence of nested encodings.

contained subtype: a form of subtype value set defined by reference to some other subtype of the same parent type, and consisting of the values of that (other) subtype.

contents (of a BER encoding): the part of the encoding which actually conveys the value.

context-specific: a class of tags used to achieve local distinctness of components of sets and sequences and choices.

D

data: (in the protocol context) the uninterpreted bits or octets conveyed between systems by some transfer mechanism.

defined context set: the set of presentation contexts available at some point in a presentation connection.

defined type (or **value**): a type (or value) provided with a reference name by a user of the notation.

delivered value: the value to which some instance of the use of a macro is defined to be equivalent.

distinguished value: an integer value provided with an identifier.

E

encoding rules: a set of rules allowing the systematic derivation of a transfer syntax from a suitably specified abstract syntax.

end-of-contents: a special marker used to indicate the end of a constructed encoding.

enumerated types: types with a finite, named, set of values.

explicit: a form of tagging in which the basic encoding rules convey the old tag together with the new.

exponent: the power to which the base is raised in expressing a real value.

export: to make a definition in some module available to the designers of other modules.

external type: a useful type which allows the embedding, within one abstract syntax value, of another value, not necessarily of an ASN.1 type, from another abstract syntax.

external reference: an explicit reference within a module to an imported definition, required only when the (macro, type, or value) reference is unambiguous.

form (of a BER encoding): whether the encoding is primitive or constructed.

generalized time type: a useful type which can be used to carry a time and date in textual form.

identifier (notation) a name given to a component of a type.

identifier (of a BER encoding) the part which conveys the tag and the form.

implicit: a form of tagging which the basic encoding rules exploit to save octets by overwriting the old tag with the new.

import: to make use, within a module, of a definition exported from some other module.

indefinite: a BER length variant which indicates that the end of the encoding is indicated by a special marker.

information: (in the protocol context) data with associated meaning.

information object: a piece of design which requires to be identified unambiguously in some instance of communication.

inner subtyping: a form of subtype value set, suitable for structured types, which includes the values whose components meet certain constraints.

integer type: a built-in type whose values are the positive and negative whole numbers and zero.

length (of a BER encoding): the part of the encoding that allows the end to be found.

long: a BER length variant used to convey the length of the contents explicitly, and which can be used for encodings of (in practice) arbitrary length.

M

macro: a user-created extension to the ASN.1 notation, allowing new syntax for types and values.

macro definition notation: the notation by which a macro is defined.

mantissa: the multiplier involved in expressing a real value.

module: a named collection of related (normally) definitions of macros, types and values.

N

null type: a built-in type containing just one value of the same name.

O

object descriptor type: a useful type whose values are textual (human-readable) identifiers of information objects.

object identifier type: a built-in type whose values are the names of the nodes of the object identifier tree.

object identifier tree: a tree formed for the purpose of naming information objects.

octet string type: a built-in type whose values are the ordered sequences of octets (8-bit bytes).

P

parent (type): a type whose values have been subsetted to form a subtype.

presentation context: an association between an abstract syntax and a transfer syntax suitable for representing its values.

presentation data value: a value of the abstract syntax associated with some presentation context.

primitive: a form of BER encoding in which the contents is a sequence of octets.

private-use: a class of tag intended to be used by one organisation to produce a private extended version of some protocol which is under the control of another.

production: a named list of alternative syntactic elements within a macro definition.

R

real type: a built-in type whose values are the real numbers approximated by rational numbers.

reference: a name given to a macro, module, production, type or value.

S

segment: a group of consecutive elements of a string, represented as one nested encoding within a constructed string encoding, whose boundaries are chosen by the sender and which have no semantic significant.

selection type: a type which is restricted to just one of the alternatives of a choice.

sequence-of type: a structured type, defined in terms of a single component type, and whose values are the (ordered) lists of values of the component type.

sequence type: a structured type which is defined in terms of a list of component types, each of whose values contains a value of each of the component types, in definition order.

set-of type: a structured type, defined in terms of a single component type, and whose values are the unordered collections of values of the component type.

set type: a structured type which is defined in terms of a collection of component types, all distinct, and each of whose values contains a value of each of the component types.

short: a BER length variant which can be used for any encoding whose contents is less than 128 octets in length.

simple type: a type whose values can be described directly, rather than in terms of other types.

single value: a form of subtype value set consisting of a particular value from the parent type.

size range: a form of subtype value set which includes all of the values whose size, measured in the appropriate units (such as bits for bit strings), is within the designated range.

structured type: a type which is defined in terms of other types - its components - and whose values are made up of values of the component types.

subtype (of a type): a type whose values are a subset of the other type.

subtype specification: notation used after type notation in order to define a new type which is a subtype of the old.

subtype value sets: some set of values from a parent type, used in a subtype specification.

T

tag: a type denotation, one or more of which are associated with every ASN.1 type, and consisting of a class and number.

tagged type: a type which is based upon another type and has the same information-bearing capacity but has a different tag.

transfer syntax: a set of (unambiguous) representations for the values in an abstract syntax.

trailing bit: the final bit in a bit string, numbered *n-1* if there are *n* bits in the string.

type: a (non-empty) set of distinct values, representing a potential for conveying information.

type assignment: a statement of ASN.1, whereby a type is given a reference name.

type notation: those sequences of ASN.1 items which denote types.

universal: a class of tags allocated to the built-in and useful types of ASN.1.

universal time type: a useful type which can be used to carry a time and date in textual form, but which is less flexible than the generalized time type, and is intended to be suitable for international applications.

useful type: a type defined in terms of the built-in types within ASN.1 itself, and which is potentially of use across a wide range of enterprises.

V

value: a particular element of a type, whose conveyance, rather than some other from that type, results in the transfer of information.

value assignment: a statement of ASN.1, whereby a value is given a reference name.

value assignment compatible: a relationship that holds between two type notations if a value defined in terms of one can be used as a value of the other.

value notation: those sequences of ASN.1 items which denote values.

value range: a form of subtype value set including all of the values of the parent type within a certain range.

Index